I lived and practiced as a ⃞⃞⃞ o
years. While there, I saw sincere meditators ⃞⃞⃞ d
attempting to undertake this beautiful but rigorous practice. I
have read or reviewed all the books in English on jhâna practice.
Jhânas Advice from Two Spiritual Friends not only provides a much-
needed bridge for a modern audience to understand and then
access these ancient practices, but it also conveys a kind of dhamma
transmission of the profoundly subtle aspects of the jhânas.

> *Robert Cusick*
> *Former Monk at Pa Auk Monastery,*
> *and Spirit Rock Manager of Retreats*

‒‒‒

Making ancient wisdom accessible to Western readers is a
delicate and demanding task, which Stephen and Tina have
done admirably. They go well beyond the text of the classical
Visuddhimagga and describe how a Theravadan master actually
taught the classical text, what blocks Westerners are likely to meet,
and how to navigate those rarely charted waters.

> *Michael Hagerty, Professor Emeritus,*
> *University of California—Davis*

‒‒‒

I am astounded by the simplicity/complexity and nuance of this practice, and that two lay Westerners have been able to both do this amazing practice and articulate it in very simple terms. I feel a sense of optimism and accessibility—as well as relief—that the practice is doable by Westerners who are not monastics. After reading this book I am both deeply touched by the very real possibility, and also inspired to explore this for myself and for the benefit of others.

Cyndia Biver
Marketing Consultant, and Spirit Rock Retreat Manager

The jhâna practice is a very important part of the Buddha's path. Ven. Pa Auk Sayadaw is recognized as one of the most rigorous jhâna teachers in the world. This book on Stephen and Tina's experience would be useful to any Buddhist who wishes to undertake the jhânas as practiced by the Buddha and taught by Ven. Pa Auk Sayadaw.

Roland K. Win
Entrepreneur, and benefactor to Ven. Pa Auk Sayadaw

JHÂNAS ADVICE
FROM TWO SPIRITUAL FRIENDS

Dear Sam,

may your path of purification
be filled with many blessings!

Steve + Tina

Venerable Pa Auk Sayadaw

Jhânas Advice from Two Spiritual Friends

Concentration Meditation as Taught by Ven. Pa Auk Sayadaw

Stephen Snyder
and
Tina Rasmussen

Kalyana Mitta Publishing
PO Box 150149
San Rafael, CA 94915

Printed in the United States of America

ISBN: 978-0-615-19876-7

CONTENTS

This book is dedicated to

the Ven. Pa Auk Sayadaw

with gratitude

ACKNOWLEDGEMENTS

First and foremost we want to thank Robert Cusick. Without him, this book would not have come into being. Robert, thank you for going to Burma and facing the challenges you encountered there, so you could bring your enthusiasm for this practice back to share with others. Thank you for introducing us to each other. You may never have thought we'd thank you for "encouraging" us (strongly) to write this book, but we are eternally grateful.

Roland Win was also a huge contributor to this book coming to fruition. His sponsorship enabled Ven. Pa Auk Sayadaw to teach the Four Springs Retreat. And, he hand carried the first draft of the manuscript to Sri Lanka himself, so that the Sayadaw could personally review it.

We also thank Kim McLaughlin for co-organizing and co-managing the Four Springs Retreat.

Many thanks to Guy Armstrong for his insight and encouragement. Guy was one of the first reviewers of the manuscript, and also introduced Tina to the jhânas practice.

We would also like to express our gratitude to the additional people who reviewed this book and gave us valuable feedback: Rick Hanson, Michael Hagerty, Cyndia Biver, and Gil Frondsal.

Thanks also to Gil for his support and guidance as we move into the role of supporting others in this practice.

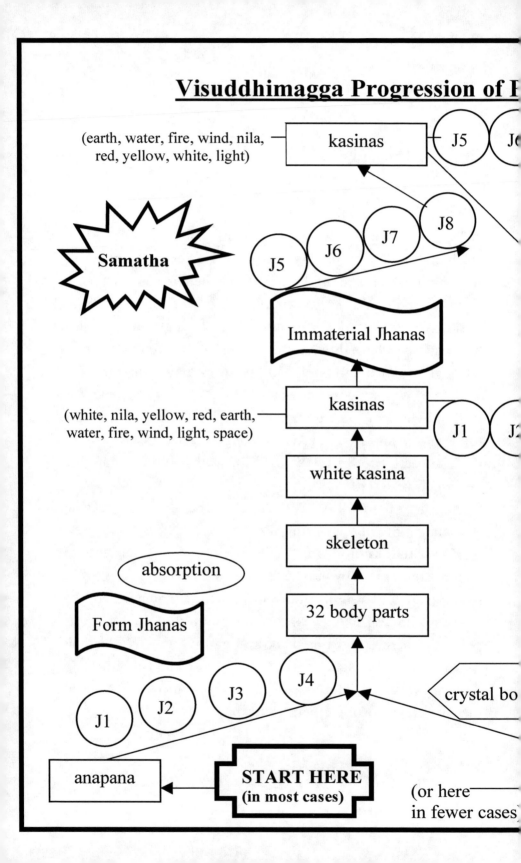

Visuddhimagga Progression of F

(earth, water, fire, wind, nila, red, yellow, white, light) — kasinas — J5 · J

Samatha

J5 · J6 · J7 · J8

Immaterial Jhanas

(white, nila, yellow, red, earth, water, fire, wind, light, space) — kasinas — J1 · J:

white kasina

skeleton

absorption

32 body parts

Form Jhanas

J1 · J2 · J3 · J4

crystal bo

anapana ← **START HERE (in most cases)** (or here in fewer cases)

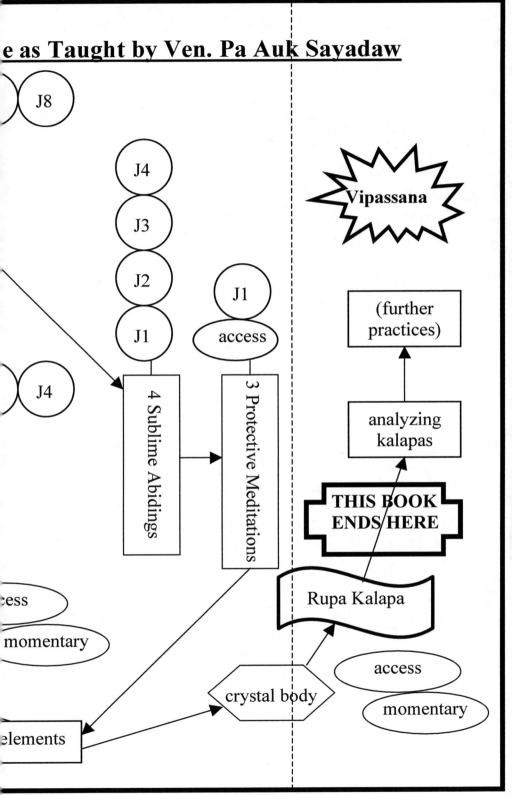

J8

J4

J3

J2

J1

J1

access

J4

Vipassana

(further practices)

4 Sublime Abidings

3 Protective Meditations

analyzing kalapas

THIS BOOK ENDS HERE

Rupa Kalapa

access

momentary

crystal body

access

momentary

elements

CHAPTER 1

WHAT ARE THE JHÂNAS, AND HOW DID WE COME TO WRITE THIS BOOK?

The story of the jhânas is a long one. It is so ancient, it pre-dates written history and even Buddhism itself. It is worth knowing, if for no other reason than to demonstrate the durability of this practice over the millennia and the worthiness of it to remain as a pillar of our modern Buddhist practices—not as a supplement or side practice, or something done for fun or for blissful spiritual experiences, but done because it has been done through the ages as a foundational method for purifying the mind.

We are not Buddhist scholars or historians. The context we provide in this chapter is a story, rather than a work of precise fact. We offer it to share what we have discovered in our own adventure to make sense of, and find the proper place for, these amazing and important practices. We also offer it to provide context to the rest of the book, which focuses solely on the practice itself—what it is actually like to practice the jhânas as a meditator.

A BRIEF STORY OF THE JHÂNAS, FROM 3000 BCE TO TODAY

In the ancient days, more than five thousand years ago (as far back as 3000 BCE), the noble ones undertook spiritual practices, as we do today. The questions were most likely the same. Who am I? Where did I come from? Why am I here? What happens when I die? Even then, people probably had rigorous debates, each side arguing the rightness of its opinion. The wise ones knew that these deep questions could only be answered through direct experience, not through intellectual speculation. So they headed for caves in the Himalayas and undertook rigorous and extraordinary practices to find out what is beyond normal perception.

After more than twenty-five hundred years of being memorized and passed down orally, in 400 BCE some of these practices were systematized and written down in one of the oldest spiritual documents known to humankind—the *Yoga Sutras of Patanjali*. Historians are not sure whether Patanjali was an individual or a lineage of yogis, or who exactly wrote them down.

These sutras focused on many things, including attachment, aversion, ethics, renunciation, meditation, and ultimately, liberation from the fetters of human suffering. A portion of the sutras focused on meditative concentration practices (called "dhyana"). These sutras were the foundational spiritual teachings of India and much of Asia for millennia, up to and including the day in which the Buddha was born. Yogis used them as their guide and basis for practice and passed them down mostly on an individual basis, from master to yogi, for thousands of years.

In 563 BCE, Siddhartha Gautama was born as the heir to the throne of a kingdom in what is now Nepal. As he came of age, he was drawn to leave his life of luxury to search for answers to the same deep questions that had drawn yogis for thousands of years away from their homes and into the life of spiritual practice. Why do we suffer, and is there any end to this suffering?

He turned to the wise ones of his day—the wandering renunciates who had also abandoned their worldly lives to seek their own direct knowledge. He was taught the well-known practices of the day, including the meditative absorptions known as jhânas. He went to various teachers to learn the jhânas progressively, finally culminating in the eighth jhâna known only to a few select teachers. (*Ariyapariyesana Sutta [The Noble Search] MN 26.*)

Once Siddhartha attained these most rigorous meditative attainments of the day, his teacher asked him to begin teaching. Five recluses with "little dust in their eyes" joined Siddhartha as he continued in his own quest in Uruvela Forest for six years. Through many tortuous mortifications he almost died but was graciously offered special milk rice from Sujata, a generous lady who was the daughter of Senani, a landowner of Seni village. At this point, he realized that extremities were not the answer—neither greedily consuming life's pleasures nor aversely pushing the world away. He determined to practice the "middle way." Later, he went to Sala forest, which is one part of Urvela forest. He practiced Samatha and Vipassana there the whole day. In the evening, he went to the Bodhi Tree, sat down under the tree, and took up his meditation object again. He practiced the whole night and attained complete liberation from suffering and the causes of suffering. At this point, at the age of thirty-five, he became "the Buddha"—the Enlightened One.

For the following forty-five years, the Buddha taught others what he learned, beginning with his five fellow students. Throughout his life, he taught people both the Samatha practices of concentration (which he defined as jhâna), as well as the Vipassana practices of insight, which went beyond what he had learned from his own teachers and led to his complete liberation under the Bodhi tree. He also continued to practice both jhâna and insight meditation. At the moment of his death, his final act was to enter jhâna.

⌐⊶

A few months after the Buddha died and the first seeds of the new religion of "Buddhism" were beginning to be planted, the Buddha's most senior followers convened to agree upon the teachings to be included as scripture. These suttas were preserved and passed down in memorized oral form.

In 250 BCE, senior Buddhist leaders became concerned about the variations that were starting to occur in the oral accounts. They decided to preserve the teachings organized as the written *Pali Cannon.* In 29 BCE, these were first put into written form in Sri Lanka, five hundred years after the Buddha's death.

Nine hundred years after the Buddha's death, a prominent and prolific Buddhist monk, commentator, and scholar—Bhadantacariya Buddhaghosa—clarified the details of exact practices. These practices were often only vaguely outlined in the suttas, which had been handed down orally for five hundred years. Buddhaghosa detailed these practices in the *Visuddhimagga (The Path of Purification)* in 430 CE.

⌐⊶

As word of the Buddha's teachings and their power spread, Buddhism began to migrate to other regions of Asia. As it moved to China, other prominent teachers added their own interpretations and teachings. The word "jhâna" or "dhyana" morphed into the word "chan'a" which eventually became "zen." The teachings of Zen spread throughout what is now China and eventually to Korea and Japan. While the meditative practices of absorption were lost, superseded by new forms of meditation, the remnant of the name remained, the jhânas hidden in obscurity.

—

In 800 CE, the king of Tibet asked a prominent yogi from present-day Pakistan to bring his spiritual practices to Tibet. The great yogi Padmasambava brought the teachings of Buddhism to this country, helping the Tibetans integrate them with their native Bon religion, as well as other advanced practices the Tibetans collected from Taoism and Ayurveda.

Initially, Tibetan cave yogis practiced jhânas as taught in India, going into full absorptions and relying on time resolves to exit from the absorption. Over time, however, numerous cave yogis were found seemingly dead, yet still alive, absorbed in jhâna. Tibetan Buddhist doctrine eventually turned away from the practice of jhâna, favoring the more engaged practices, meditating with eyes open. "Break the meditation" became the instruction, discouraging practitioners from entering absorption at any time.

—

Buddhism increased in popularity, flourishing under the reign of King Ashoka in 261 BCE, who used his wide power and influence to establish monasteries and teaching schools throughout Asia and even in the West as far as Greece. Various lineages of Buddhism sprung up. The original school, which adhered primarily to the teachings of the Buddha himself, was now called Theravada Buddhism ("the way of the elders"). For hundreds of years,

Buddhism flourished and evolved into many forms.

In 1100 CE, however, with the rise of other competing religions, Buddhism began to decline in its original homeland, with the ransacking of monasteries and the loss of adherents. By 1400, Theravada Buddhism was the primary religion only in the few countries of Southeast Asia: Sri Lanka, Laos, Cambodia, Thailand, and Burma.

In 1934, the boy Acinna was born in Leigh-Chaung Village about one hundred miles northwest of Yangon, Myanmar (Burma). At the age of ten, he ordained as a novice (samanera) in his village. Later at the age of twenty, he was ordained as a full-fledged monk, a Bhikkhu. As a samanera and as a Bhikkhu, he was trained under the guidance of learned elder monks, completing the prestigious Dhammacariya examination in 1954 (the equivalent of a Master's degree in Buddhist Pali Studies).

For the next eight years, he traveled throughout Myanmar to learn from various well-known Buddhist teachers. In 1964, he began "forest dwelling" in order to intensify his meditation practice. For the next sixteen years, he made forest dwelling his primary practice, living a simple life of intensive meditation and scriptural study.

In 1981, Ven. Acinna received a message from Ven. Aggapanna, the abbot of Pa-Auk Forest Monastery. Ven. Aggapanna was dying, and asked Ven. Acinna to look after the monastery. Five days later, Ven. Aggapanna died and Ven. Acinna became known as Ven. Pa Auk Tawya Sayadaw, the new abbot. Although he oversaw monastery operations, he spent most of his time in seclusion, meditating in a bamboo hut in the upper forest.

Foreign meditators began arriving at the monastery in the early

1990s, as the Sayadaw's reputation grew. In 1997, the Ven. Pa Auk Sayadaw wrote his Magnum Opus, the enormous five-volume tome in Burmese titled *The Practice that Leads to Nibanna*, explaining the entire course of teaching in detail, supported by copious quotations from the Pali texts (of which he is fluent). In 1999, in public recognition of his achievements, the Burmese government bestowed upon him the title of "Highly Respected Meditation Teacher." In 1999, Ven. Pa Auk Sayadaw wrote *Knowing and Seeing* (also available in English) which is a shorter 350-page version of this path of practice, including extensive instruction on the form and formless jhânas.

The monastery expanded from a simple bamboo hut and a handful of disciples to housing for more than eight hundred full-time monastic and lay practitioners, four meditation halls, a library, a clinic, a hospital, and an almsgiving hall. In March 2007, more than 130 foreign monastics and lay practitioners resided at Pa Auk Monastery. During the rains retreat, the population in 2007 averaged eight to nine hundred and often exceeded fifteen hundred people during festivals.

Meanwhile in the United States, in 1976, four American friends established the Insight Meditation Society (IMS) in Barre, Massachusetts, after studying Theravada Buddhism in Southeast Asia. Joseph Goldstein, Jack Kornfield, Sharon Salzburg, and Jacqueline Schwartz studied with numerous teachers and brought these teachings (primarily focusing on Vipassana Insight mindfulness meditation in the lineage of Ven. Mahasi Sayadaw) back to the West. As some of the first Westerners teaching Buddhism, the spread of the practices were gradual and sometimes slow. But with persistence and dedication, the sangha grew. *(The Faces of*

Buddhism in America, by Charles S. Prebish and Kenneth K. Tanaka; Chapter 9, *Insight Meditation in the United States: Life, Liberty, and the Pursuit of Happiness* by Gil Fronsdal; University of California Press, Berkeley and Los Angeles, 1998.)

In 1981, Ven. Mahasi Sayadaw came to IMS to officially certify the center as an Insight Meditation Center in his tradition. In 1987, Jack Kornfield directed the purchase of the land for Spirit Rock Retreat Center in Woodacre, California.

Together, in 2007 Spirit Rock and IMS hosted more than forty thousand meditators, some completing retreats as long as two or three months. IMS and Spirit Rock continue to host the most respected Asian Theravada teachers, including Ven. Pa Auk Sayadaw and many others.

➴

In 1976, in a suburb of Chicago, Illinois, at the age of thirteen, Tina Rasmussen learned to meditate and began practicing. The same year, in San Francisco, California, at the age of nineteen, Stephen Snyder became interested in Zen Buddhism and began a daily meditation practice.

➴

In early 2003, Robert Cusick—a student of Gil Fronsdal (founder of the Insight Meditation Center in Redwood City, California)—ventured to Pa Auk Monastery in Burma to ordain as a Buddhist monk. In 2004, he returned to the United States as a lay practitioner, full of enthusiasm and in awe of Ven. Pa Auk Sayadaw, and what he knew of the Sayadaw's teachings.

One day in early summer 2004 after his return from Burma, Robert was having tea with a woman he had met at a social gathering a few weeks before. She had undergone a profound experience practicing the jhânas under the guidance of Guy Armstrong, and was interested in studying with Ven. Pa Auk Sayadaw to understand more about what had happened. She wanted to hear more of Robert's experiences, as she was planning to attend the Sayadaw's first U.S. retreat in 2005.

In the middle of their intense discussion, they realized their parking meters were about to expire, so they walked to her car to put in more quarters. Robert was going to meet a friend for lunch and coincidentally, the friend had parked right behind the woman's car in front of Open Secret Books in San Rafael, California.

The three of them happened to be there at the same moment, and Stephen and Tina met for the first time. Robert, Stephen, and Tina decided to have lunch together. Six weeks later, in August of 2004, Tina and Stephen were married.

⌐⊸

In March and April of 2005, Ven. Pa Auk Sayadaw held his first retreat in America. Robert was one of the co-organizers along with Kim McLaughlin, and Stephen and Tina attended along with about thirty other practitioners.

The retreat was held at the Four Springs Retreat Center near Middletown, California. Approximately fifty people attended the retreat, most of them for the entire two months. Lay people and monastics came from as far as Bali and Taiwan to attend. On the second day of the retreat, Tina ordained as a Theravada nun, had her head shaved, and took on the robes and the monastic vows. Ven. Pa Auk Sayadaw gave her the dharma name of Ayya Pesala.

Conditions were difficult, with cold, wet weather, minimal heating, and no food after noon each day. Long lines formed in the rain outside the Sayadaw's cottage, as meditators waited every day or two to report on their meditation practice and receive instruction.

Throughout the retreat, the Sayadaw's warmth, determination, and commitment to participants' liberation were always apparent in the long hours he made himself available for private instruction and talks, despite the demands on his health. His tireless dedication to the Buddha's teaching based on his meditative experience and extensive study of the scriptures was uncompromising. And, his unrelenting pace was driven by his heartfelt, compassionate intention for all beings to complete the Buddha's path. When a student completed one attainment, Ven. Pa Auk Sayadaw smiled and then immediately gave instructions for the next.

In April 2005, Tina became the first Western woman and first American to attain the eight jhânas in the lineage of Ven. Pa Auk Sayadaw, and Stephen became the second Western layman and first American male to attain the eight jhânas in the lineage of Ven. Pa Auk Sayadaw.

━

As the retreat approached its end, the Sayadaw strongly and frequently encouraged people to come back with him to Burma to continue the practice. Later in 2005, Robert returned to Burma for another year as a monk at Pa Auk Monastery.

In the spring of 2006, Ven. Pa Auk Sayadaw offered another two-month jhâna retreat in the West, this time at the Forest Refuge in Barre, Massachusetts.

━

In early summer 2007, Stephen had lunch with Robert and a friend of Robert's, who had also been a monk at Pa Auk Monastery. Through the former monks' questions, Stephen could see their strong interest in the traditional practice of jhâna as preserved by the Ven. Pa Auk Sayadaw. He also saw the growing need for clarifying information on jhâna, presented specifically for modern practitioners. After the lunch, Stephen decided to document his experience of the jhâna retreat with Ven. Pa Auk Sayadaw. Tina joined in this process a few months later.

This book is the result. It is intended to serve as a bridge between the traditional, esoteric, and rigorous jhâna teaching as found in Ven. Pa Auk Sayadaw's book *Knowing and Seeing* (which provides scriptural authority and traditional instructions) and modern practitioners who are drawn to this noble and ancient practice that was such an integral component of the Buddha's own path of purification leading to liberation.

At the writing of this book, the Ven. Pa Auk Sayadaw is seventy-three years old. At this time, he is considered the leading Asian master teaching the jhâna practices, in addition to the teaching of the insight practices of Vipassana. Now is the time to learn this ancient and worthy practice, before it is lost to obscurity.

When the Sayadaw was young, his teacher told him it was his charge to plant the seeds of his teaching in the West. Despite his advancing age, he continues to travel around the world to offer these teachings, preserving them and passing them on.

CHAPTER 2

PREPARING FOR JHÂNAS: PRELIMINARY PRACTICES AND FOUNDATIONAL UNDERSTANDINGS

For those desiring to emulate the meditative path of the historical Buddha Shakyamuni, there can be little question that a pursuit of jhâna is warranted. The experience of many modern Buddhist adherents is that the demanding requirements of practicing the jhânas according to the suttas and the Visuddhimagga make it a lofty goal, out of actual reach. (The Visuddhimagga [Seattle, WA: Buddhist Publication Society, Pariyatti Editions, 1991] is a treatise of Theravada Buddhism. It was written in the fifth century as an organized compilation of the Buddha's teachings in the Pali Cannon, in the form of a detailed meditation manual.) In the West, it is often believed that it is unlikely, if not impossible, to attain the jhânas as described in the more detailed instructions outlined in the Visuddhimagga (which have the suttas as their foundation). Nonetheless, with a proper presentation of the historical basis for jhâna coupled with firsthand experiential pointers, the modern seeker can have at hand the tools to undertake jhâna practice as taught by Ven. Pa Auk Sayadaw.

The Buddha unintentionally entered jhâna when first meditating as a very young boy. "I recall once when my father the Shakyan was working, and I was sitting in the cool shade of a rose-apple tree, then quite withdrawn from sensuality, withdrawn from unskillful mental qualities—I entered and remained in the first jhâna" (*Mahasaccaka Sutta MN 36*).

At that time, nearly twenty-six hundred years ago, jhâna practice was widespread. Upon undertaking the ascetic life in search of spiritual awakening, the Buddha became experientially familiar with the jhânas (*Mahasaccaka Sutta MN 36*).

The Buddha extensively referenced jhâna practice as an essential part of the Buddhist path. In fact, entering jhâna was not only the Buddha's final meditative practice, but it was also the final action of his life.

> Then the Blessed One addressed the monks, "Now then, [monastics], I extort you: All fabrications are subject to decay. Bring about completion by being heedful." Those were the Tathagata's last words. Then the Blessed One entered the first jhâna. (*MahaParinibbana Sutta, DN 16*)

His final action was to sequentially enter each of the jhânas from the first through the eighth (four form jhânas and four formless jhânas). He then descended from the eighth jhâna in reverse order to the first jhâna. The Buddha then entered the first, second, third, and fourth form jhâna. "Emerging from the fourth jhâna, he immediately was totally unbound." (*MahaParinibbana Sutta, DN 16*)

Clearly, the Buddha was a supremely attained meditator. He

could have elected to do any of a number of sophisticated spiritual practices at the time of his death. That he entered jhâna as his last act supports the conclusion of the importance of jhâna.

⟶

There are presently in the West a number of teachers offering jhâna retreats and teachings. There is not a uniformity of presentation of jhâna teachings. While there may be many approaches to the jhâna practice, this book focuses on jhânas as referenced in numerous suttas of the Buddha and detailed more specifically in the *Visuddhimagga (The Path of Purification)* as presented and taught by the Ven. Pa Auk Sayadaw of Pa Auk Monastery, Myanmar (Burma). This book is designed to be used in conjunction with Ven. Pa Auk Sayadaw's very detailed and specific explanations of every step of the practice, as found in his book *Knowing and Seeing* (Kuala Lumpur, Malaysia: WAVE Publications, 2003). We will not repeat the details that he provides in this text.

The jhâna pointers contained in this book are our direct experiences, the experiences of two Western practitioners who completed the eight jhânas (four form jhânas and four formless jhânas) and related practices under the personal and rigorous guidance of Ven. Pa Auk Sayadaw on a two-month retreat in Middletown, California, in March and April of 2005. We believe the principal reason these very rigorous jhânas have been so challenging a practice for modern yogis is due to confusion about the practical steps necessary for attainment, as well as a misapplication of the concentrated meditative energy. It is our hope that these are remedied, at least partially, herein.

In this chapter, we will discuss the wholesome base of preliminary practices that support jhâna meditation practice, as well as other foundational topics, including silence, breathing, and effort. We will also discuss the types of concentration, momentary and access concentration as a precursor to jhâna, and the function of nimitta leading to absorption.

Throughout, we will share our relevant experiences and provide suggestions that may be helpful to the jhâna practitioner. We want to be clear that we are not Buddhist scholars or historians. We are dedicated practitioners and yogis. We apologize for any omissions in scholarly context. The Ven. Pa Auk Sayadaw does a wonderful job of referencing specific scriptures in his book *Knowing and Seeing*, so we encourage you to read his book for more detailed information. We also encourage you to read the suttas and the *Visuddhimagga* directly, to see for yourself what the ancients and noble ones said about these practices. Our focus here is on the practice itself, as we experienced it. We offer this as a guide to others in furtherance of their own direct experience.

THE THREE STAGES OF PRACTICE

We would like to begin by setting this book in the context of the entire path of practice as outlined by the Buddha and set forth in the Theravada tradition. The path to liberation includes three stages:

- Ethical behavior or morality (Sila)
- Concentration or serenity (Samatha)
- Insight (Vipassana)

Ethical behavior lays the foundation for the other practices. We will outline the foundation of Sila as taught in Theravada Buddhism briefly in the next few pages.

The majority of this book focuses on the Samatha practice, of which the jhâna practice is a part. Samatha is also referred to as the "path of purification." In undertaking jhâna practice, the yogi inevitably encounters hindrances and attachments. While these may seem like obstacles to the practice, working with them actually *is* the practice, when one understands that Samatha is designed for purification of mind. How do you know if you are "doing" the practice? Often, we know because we are encountering hindrances. This is, in fact, engaging the practice of purifying the mind.

Vipassana is the third segment of the Buddha's teachings, and is often called the "path of insight." Through Vipassana practices, and as one's meditative capacity deepens, it is possible to see directly into the nature of reality, beyond what is available in normal perception.

Ven. Pa Auk Sayadaw teaches all three aspects of practice. In our study with him, we focused primarily on what we are presenting in this book. For this reason, we will not be detailing the other aspects of the Buddha's path as taught by Ven. Pa Auk Sayadaw. His book *Knowing and Seeing* is an excellent reference that details not only the Samatha portion of the path, but also Vipassana.

PRELIMINARY PRACTICES OF SILA

PRECEPTS

Jhânas are a highly specialized meditative undertaking. Daily Samatha practice can be a wonderful means for cultivating serenity, developing concentration, and beginning to purify the mind. For an in-depth exploration of the practice, the yogi should devote a minimum of ten days to several months. Prior to beginning a jhâna retreat, it is beneficial for the student to undertake daily meditation practice, and to develop the moral ground from which jhâna exploration can most readily commence.

Ven. Pa Auk Sayadaw requires the practitioner undertaking

a jhâna retreat to take the Eight Precepts, or at a minimum the Five Precepts. The precepts are taken as an act of virtue, a wholesomeness of person, intention and spirit. Wholesomeness promotes successful Ânàpànàsati Meditation and eventually jhâna. Ideally the meditator undertakes these precepts in anticipation of the jhâna retreat. Inviting wholesomeness and turning away from unwholesome thoughts and actions is absolutely vital to purifying the mind. If a meditator is too distracted by attractions and aversions, a jhâna retreat is not as productive as it could be. This is not meant to convey that anyone who is not successful on a jhâna retreat is unwholesome. There are numerous counterproductive actions that may appear harmless to the normal meditator. Particularly judging oneself and others on the retreat in any manner is a block to this sensitive meditation. The precepts must be allowed into our deepest level of intention and aspiration. The spirit and meaning of the precepts must be honored in cultivating the ground for jhâna practice.

EIGHT PRECEPTS

1. I undertake the precept to refrain from destroying living creatures.
2. I undertake the precept to refrain from taking that which is not given.
3. I undertake the precept to refrain from all sexual activity.
4. I undertake the precept to refrain from incorrect speech.
5. I undertake the precept to refrain from intoxicating drinks and drugs that lead to carelessness.
6. I undertake to refrain from eating at the forbidden time (i.e., after twelve noon).
7. I undertake the precept to refrain from dancing, singing, listening to music, going to see entertainment, wearing garlands, using perfumes, and beautifying the body with

cosmetics.

8. I undertake the precept to refrain from lying on a high or luxurious seat or sleeping place.

(Incorrect speech is defined in the *Magga-vibhanga Sutta* as "abstaining from lying, abstaining from divisive speech, abstaining from abusive speech, abstaining from idle chatter" [SN 45.8].) As mentioned later, idle chatter, both external and internal, needs to be silenced during a jhâna retreat.

These precepts are usually taken at the commencement of a jhâna retreat. To the extent possible, honoring and applying as many of the precepts prior to the retreat lays the wholesome groundwork for purification of mind as found in the jhâna practice. A wholesome mind expresses wholesome actions.

For practitioners undertaking the jhâna practice, the precepts can be modified to fit the life of a householder, as is common in the West. For example, the precepts can be used as below, while living a worldly life. Undertaking these practices on an ongoing basis, in preparation for a retreat, or on retreat can help one engage in Sila.

FIVE PRECEPTS

1. I undertake the precept to refrain from harming living creatures.
2. I undertake the precept to refrain from taking that which is not given.
3. I undertake the precept to refrain from harming others through sexual activity.
4. I undertake the precept to refrain from incorrect speech.
5. I undertake the precept to refrain from clouding the mind through consuming intoxicating drinks and drugs that lead to carelessness.

FOUR NOBLE TRUTHS

The seminal teaching of the Buddha is the Four Noble Truths. These are:

1. That there is suffering in life.
2. The origin of suffering.
3. The cessation of suffering.
4. The way to the cessation of suffering.

The noble truths are the subject of extensive teaching in Buddhism. In summary, suffering can be viewed as grasping or rejecting what is occurring. This suffering manifests as desiring something that we do not obtain, or receiving the object desired and then either losing it, or wanting more than was received. The origin of suffering is complex. Simply put, it is the belief in an identity separate from the awakening mind stream of the unconditioned. This imagined identity then seeks itself both internally and externally. Also, this sense of a separate self takes the thoughts to be coming from an identity. Cessation of suffering, as taught by the Buddha, is living a balanced life through the Eightfold Path.

EIGHTFOLD PATH (FROM DHAMMACAKKAPPAVATTANA SUTTA—SN 56.11)

1. Right view
2. Right intention
3. Right speech
4. Right action
5. Right livelihood
6. Right effort
7. Right mindfulness

8. Right concentration

The last of the eightfold path—right concentration—is defined repeatedly by the Buddha as jhâna. (See *Magga-vibhanga SN 45.8; See also Mahasatipatthana Sutta DN 22.*)

FOUNDATIONAL UNDERSTANDINGS

The sections that follow are presented to provide a context for the practitioner in understanding some of the most important foundations for the initial access and prolonged availability of the jhânas.

JHÂNA FACTORS

The five jhâna factors are:

1. Applied attention (*vitakka*)
2. Sustained attention (*vicâra*)
3. Joy (*piti*)
4. Bliss (*sukha*)
5. One-pointedness (*ekaggatâ*)

Vitakka is translated as applied attention. This is the initial movement of attention to the meditative object. This object will vary throughout the progression of practice, from the breath to the kasinas to other objects. The first practice one undertakes will be Ânàpànàsati Meditation, which means "mindfulness of breathing." The object for this practice is the *awareness* of the *sensation* of the *movement* of the breath as it crosses the "ânàpàna spot." (The *ânàpàna spot* is a term we are using for the location of the meditator's attention on the spot below the nose on the upper lip where the breath crosses.) For example when you find your attention has wandered from the breath crossing the ânàpàna spot, it is gently directed back. Each time the attention wanders, it is nonjudgmentally returned to the object.

Vicâra is translated as sustained attention. As the attention stays with the object, an infusion of continuous uninterrupted attention develops. As the meditative attention does not wander from the object for thirty minutes, vicâra becomes stronger and is more noticeable. Vicâra strengthens by maintaining the attention on the breath crossing the ânàpàna spot while in meditation posture as well as when walking, eating, showering, and moving around.

Attention should never waver from the object when the student is doing jhâna practice. It is a kind of love affair with the object, which initially is the breath as it crosses the ânàpàna spot. The meditator applies and sustains attention constantly throughout the day. Before, during, and after each and every inhalation, pause, and exhalation, the attention is on the breath as it crosses the ânàpàna spot. On a jhâna retreat, while doing the Ânàpànàsati Meditation practice, the student never, never, never takes the attention off of the breath crossing the ânàpàna spot. Every activity is done *while simultaneously* placing attention on the object.

Think of the metaphor of balancing a spoon on the end of your nose. Throughout every activity of the day and night, the student is trying to maintain the spoon balanced on the nose. Should the spoon slip off, it is placed back on the nose and the attention stays exactly on the spot where the spoon merges with skin. When attention is applied and sustained on the object, the jhâna factors arise naturally.

Piti translates as joy. We have found the term "joy" to be a little difficult for some students to differentiate from other pleasant or happy feelings. Piti, as experienced, feels like happiness in the body, not a happy thought. It seems to be felt in the body, although it is actually a mentally induced state. Sometimes it is referred to as "rapture." If a meditator is struggling with restlessness, piti can be sought in the body. The student scans the body looking for a bodily felt experience of mentally produced joy. Conversely, because piti can be so intense in the body, at times it can cause restlessness. This grosser aspect of piti becomes beneficial as one progresses through the jhânas, because it allows for gradual nonattachment to pleasant experiences.

Sukha is used in jhâna practice to mean bliss. Bliss is a tricky word. There are so many meanings and implications. Sukha is best understood as a mentally sensed bliss that is also felt subtly in the body. While piti could be experienced as body happiness, sukha can be experienced more like gentle contentment. Sukha is more settled and refined in its feeling than piti. Piti is more excitable in its feeling and somewhat more gross. Again, both are produced mentally.

Ekaggatâ is described as one-pointedness of mind. The sense of this mental state is of a focusing of attention and intention. It is a collecting and unification of meditative energy. There is an experience of uninterrupted unification with the meditative object. Think of a flashlight that can be adjusted to a wider or narrower beam of light. When the beam of light is narrowed to the visual width of a pencil and the functioning of a laser—this would be analogous to ekaggatâ in jhâna practice. It is a cohering of the attention.

In the first jhâna, the above five jhâna factors are present. However, as the meditator progresses to the fourth jhâna, the factor of *upekkhâ* (equanimity) arises in addition to replace the feeling of sukha (bliss). A "feeling" mental state is ever present in all mind moments and all of the jhânas, up through the eighth jhâna. Because of this, the above five jhâna factors are given to denote first jhâna only. (Upekkhâ will be described further in the section on the fourth jhâna.)

As concentration develops, the jhâna factors naturally arise on their own. The student cannot stay with the object while simultaneously searching for each jhâna factor. Because this splits the attention and weakens concentration, if prolonged, there is insufficient meditative energy for the jhâna factors to develop. For this reason, the meditator should only check the jhâna factors infrequently.

The jhâna factors arise as concentration meditation deepens. When the jhâna factors are present, the meditator is close to *nimitta* presenting. (The *nimitta* is a light that appears when concentration deepens and the jhâna factors are gaining strength. Nimitta is discussed in detail later.)

The Ven. Pa Auk Sayadaw teaches that the student *never* takes a jhâna factor as an object of meditation to progress toward absorption/jhâna. The jhâna factors should be considered to be the force that mysteriously opens the student to jhâna, not the object of jhâna meditation. To progress toward the first jhâna during Ânàpànàsati Meditation, the *knowing* of the *sensation* of the *movement* of the breath crossing the ânàpàna spot is *always and only* the object of concentration. To focus on any other object is to erode concentration and decrease the likelihood of the first jhâna arising. Concentration wanes *every time* attention is taken off of the object.

Some modern Western teachings encourage one to take jhâna factors as the object. Even in the suttas, with certain translations and the seeming vagueness of the instructions, it can sound as though the suttas refer to taking jhâna factors as an object. Common knowledge of absorptions in the Buddha's day may have minimized the necessity for him to give detailed instructions on jhânas, as the instructions were likely to be well known to people of his time. However, if one reviews the *Visuddhimagga,* which has much more detailed instructions, it clearly states that one continues with the primary object to maintain the integrity of the concentration all the way into absorption. Ven. Pa Auk Sayadaw also explicitly instructs not to turn away from the breath as it crosses the ânàpàna spot at *any time* during Ânàpànàsati Meditation. One may briefly check the jhâna factors to determine which jhâna is present, but this is done only briefly.

In our experience, using the jhâna factors as an object is very, very pleasant but only leads to an intense access concentration. This is because as one progresses through the four jhânas (or even greater numbers of jhânas once the kasina practice begins) and the jhâna factors drop one by one, the meditator would need to change the primary object several times in rapid succession and in a short amount of time. Concentration, by definition, is a unification of attention. The most effective way attention can be unified is to stay with one object throughout the practice.

HINDRANCES

Hindrances prevent us from practicing effectively. The five hindrances are:

- sensual desire
- ill will
- sloth and torpor
- restlessness and remorse
- doubt

Briefly, sensual desire is seeking pleasant experiences through the "five strings of sensuality" of touch, taste, smell, sight, and hearing. (See the *Maha-durrhaknjandha Sutta M13, Ariyapariyesana*

Sutta M26, and *Bahuvedaniya Sutta M59.*) Ill will can include anger, or judgment of ourselves, others, or an event. It can also take the form of aversion, including dislike and fear. Sloth is often used to describe sluggishness, while torpor is more a drowsy mind state. Restlessness is an unsettled mental state. Remorse is the sense of regretting our past actions. Doubt can show itself as distrust in our teacher, the teachings, or our ability to meditate properly and effectively.

The Ven. Pa Auk Sayadaw instructs students that the five jhâna factors are a wholesome medicine for the five hindrances. As the student turns away from the hindrances and turns toward the jhâna factors, the hindrances recede and the jhâna factors increase, arising simultaneously. The five jhâna factors are:

1. Applied attention (*vitakka*)
2. Sustained attention (*vicâra*)
3. Joy (*piti*)
4. Bliss (*sukha*)
5. One-pointedness (*ekaggatâ*)

Early in a retreat, most, if not all, meditators are likely to experience one or more of the hindrances. We found that guarding the sense doors by keeping our vision mostly downward while fostering compassion and lovingkindness for ourselves and others helps considerably. Also, one can develop a kind of love for the meditative object and the timeless deep silence and stillness that are ever present. Perhaps this depth of silence and the accompanying accepting contentedness is a balm for the outbreak of hindrances. The meditator can take refuge in the pristine silence of the practice.

When any of the hindrances arise, the student should determine which hindrance is present. Heartfelt compassion for the hindrance and ourselves is a vital first step. Once we have met the hindrance with kind compassion, we should apply the jhâna factor to the specific hindrance. For example, if restlessness is arising routinely enough to be a distraction, the student should begin specifically cultivating bliss. Bliss is the antidote to restlessness. A discussion of the experiential characteristics of each jhâna factor can be found below. The Buddha discussed starving the hindrances and feeding the factors of awakening in the *Ahara Sutta, SN 46.51.*

Each jhâna factor neutralizes a specific hindrance:

1. Applied attention (*vitakka*) calms sensual desire.
2. Sustained attention (*vicâra*) pacifies ill will.
3. Joy (*piti*) vanquishes sloth and torpor.
4. Bliss (*sukha*) eliminates restlessness and remorse.
5. One-pointedness (*ekaggatâ*) overcomes doubt.

SILENCE

Probably the single largest impediment to successful jhâna practice is talking. The busy everyday mind must still to the point that external *and* internal talking cease. If there is even the slightest amount of talking during this concentrated period, the accumulated meditative energy begins to dissipate. While it may seem insignificant to talk a little on retreat, the amount of concentration that burns off in talking even a small amount could be enough to prevent jhâna from arising. We strongly encourage you to make the most of your many hours of sitting by maintaining a pristine container and allowing other practitioners to do the same.

Conversely, some practitioners maintain outer silence without silencing inner talk. Inner talk can take many forms. For some people it is a running commentary on life experiences and memories. Others may also find constant evaluating and judging of the meditation's development to be a temptation for inner talk. *All of these must become silent.* Another way of framing this is to "renounce thinking" for the period of the retreat.

We find that maintaining a vigilant awareness of inner talk is a vital first step. You cannot influence what you do not see. The watching of inner chatter is not to judge or condemn ourselves. The ordinary mind is watched with patient persistence. An attitude of loving compassion is the best salve when the inner chatter begins. Perhaps a blend of turning away from the chatter coupled with compassion for its arising is the best approach. At each developing stage of the Ânàpànàsati Meditation practice, its best to allow your awareness to rest in the silence that is always present. As concentration develops, the silence becomes more and more of a magnet. Later, the inner thoughts and outer words drop away and the silence that precedes thought and expression of words is present.

When beginning a jhâna retreat, direct the attention to the breath as it crosses the ânàpàna spot, on the upper lip just under the nose, to the exclusion of your internal chatter. Do not try to stop the mental chatter; simply do not give it *extra* energy by commenting upon it. Commenting on the inner chatter leads to judgments about the chatter and to new comments on the judging itself. This naturally compounds the distraction from a passing issue to a time-consuming diversion.

As the meditation periods lengthen from forty-five minutes to several hours, the mind settles and the talking becomes subtle, sometimes to the point of stopping. Longer periods of meditation are possible as the jhâna factors of piti and sukha increase and offset physical or mental stress or pain normally present. Inner chatter and thinking may diminish to the extent of simply being of no interest.

In our experience, the inner mind chatter did stop. As the silence deepens, any movement of the mind toward thinking is uncomfortable—almost unbearable. In the few instances when Stephen experienced the mind turning toward its chatter, after deep settling had begun, he was slightly nauseous, almost seasick. The process of thinking after the silence has become dominant feels very coarse energetically. Turning from deep-seated silence to inner or outer talking is not desirable. In fact, we found that when other retreatants tried to talk to us, it was almost painful. We felt conflicted between wanting to engage with others at a personal level and sustaining the pristine concentration. Eventually, we avoided contact despite how others may have perceived this.

If held in a pristine state, the dominant orientation of the meditative mind at this stage of silence is toward deeper and deeper silence. It becomes a reinforcing process.

We found that there is a kind of energy or impulse prior to thinking. As the mind settled, thinking felt uncomfortably coarse. These pre-thinking impulses were sufficient information to know how to get up, serve oneself a meal, use the toilet, and so on. It felt as though the impulse toward food, sleep, etc., could be acted upon without directing the impulse to develop into a thought. It was reassuring to find that one can function normally without the usual experience of thinking or internal commentary.

DEVELOPING MEDITATIVE CONCENTRATION ON "THE ÂNÀPÀNÀ SPOT"

While the *Visuddhimagga* references forty Samatha meditation objects, the preferred initial meditative object for Samatha practice is mindfulness of breathing (ânàpànàsati), as described in the *Mahsatipatthana Sutta DN 22.*

Ven. Pa Auk Sayadaw includes the above-referenced sutta and gives the instruction on the Ânàpànàsati Meditation practice from his book *Knowing and Seeing* (pp. 19–20). It is paraphrased as follows:

> Monastics—here in this teaching, a monastic, having gone to the forest or to the foot of a tree or to an empty place, sits down cross-legged and keeps the body erect and establishes mindfulness on the meditative object; only mindfully one breathes in and only mindfully one breathes out.

1. Breathing in a long breath one knows, "I am breathing in a long breath," or breathing out a long breath one knows, "I am breathing out a long breath."
2. Breathing in a short breath one knows, "I am breathing in a short breath," or breathing out a short breath one knows, "I am breathing out a short breath."
3. "Experiencing the whole breath body I breathe in," thus one trains oneself, and, "Experiencing the whole breath body I breathe out," thus one trains oneself.
4. "Calming the breath body I breathe in," thus one trains oneself, and "Calming the breath body I breathe out," thus one trains oneself. (*See DN 22.*)

As presented by Ven. Pa Auk Sayadaw, the instruction given is to know the breath as it enters and leaves the body at the point below the nostrils. The entire breath of inhalation, pause, exhalation, pause, is what is referred to as the "whole breath body." The entire breath body is sensed/watched *only* at the ānàpàna spot, the point on the upper lip directly below the nose. The breath should *not* be followed into or away from the body.

With the attention on the breath crossing the ānàpàna spot, it is the *sensation of movement* of the breath that is the object here—*not* the skin. The attention is placed on the small, subtle sensation where the movement of breath is detected as it goes in and out of the nostrils. This is very important! If one does not follow the instructions specifically, the nimitta will *never* merge with the breath at the ânàpàna spot. As described later, this merging is essential for absorption into the first jhâna. Without it, first jhâna absorption will *not* happen, although momentary and even access concentration is possible.

The movement and sensation of breath at the ânàpàna spot is not evaluated, judged, or controlled. Allowing one's natural breath is important. The meditator's attention should *never* leave this object. During the meditation period, the attention must be placed back on the breath as it passes the specified spot, as often as it wanders away. When the attention wavers or wanders from the object, it should be gently returned without critique or judgment of any kind.

When the retreatant is not meditating, the attention should *always* remain on the breath crossing the ânàpàna spot. With each breath taken, the meditator's attention is first and foremost on this object. During every action, whether it be walking, eating, or showering, attention should be established on the breath crossing the ânàpàna spot. During the night upon slight waking, place the attention on this object. Immediately upon waking up in the morning, place and sustain the attention on the knowing of the sensation of the movement of breath as it crosses the ânàpàna spot. If the attention wavers at any time, gently return it to the object. In this way over a suitable period of time, the jhâna factors arise and the attention merges with the object. Around this time the mind settles enough to extend meditation periods up to several hours, fostering arising of the nimitta.

BREATHING

The breath is the cornerstone of the Ânàpànàsati Meditation practice. To begin a meditation period with a few deep breaths helps draw the attention to the breath crossing the ânàpàna spot. After a few breaths, no effort is made to direct the breath. Usually the meditator is aware of each breath's duration. For Stephen, monitoring whether the breath was long or short was not helpful, but counting was initially useful. For Tina, using the traditional counting of one through eight or noticing (not noting as self-talk but simply noticing) whether the breath was short or long initially deepened concentration. Later, this was not necessary and could be dropped. Whatever the duration of the breath, the meditator maintains the attention on the breath as it crosses the ânàpàna spot. As the breath moves in an inhalation or exhalation, the attention remains fixed on the object. The attention remains on this object even when there is little or no breath. The attitude is one of waiting for the sensation of movement of breath crossing at the ânàpàna spot.

As first jhâna is reached, followed by second, third, and fourth jhânas, the breath becomes more and more discrete. There is some discussion as to whether the breath actually stops. We would say that the breath becomes very, very subtle and *feels* like it has stopped, although we cannot explain how this is physically possible. The Ven. Pa Auk Sayadaw instructs that the breath in the fourth jhâna does indeed stop, citing the *Rahogata Sutta*. When the beginning student checks for breath, this checking or investigating mind is outside the fourth jhâna. The investigating mind and full absorption in fourth jhâna cannot coexist simultaneously. The investigating mind does produce a very, very subtle breath. Due to very strong concentration, the beginning student may not realize she or he is shifting from fourth jhâna absorption concentration to the investigating mind, as it may occur in an instant. Because the shift can be so quick, it can *appear* to the beginning student that there is a continuity of breath in fourth jhâna. In either case, the body and mind can sometimes experience a surge of fright at cognizing the possibility of insufficient breath to keep the body alive. The experience of bodily fright is fairly normal. It is important, however, to not give in to the sense of panic by taking a large breath at the time of fright or by continuing to investigate this phenomenon. Doing either of these will diminish concentration. The meditator is then set back in her or his effort to still the mind enough for deep concentration to lead to nimitta and jhâna. It's best to trust the process as it unfolds.

As the Ânàpànàsati Meditation practice deepens, the pause between breaths may become longer. The student maintains the attention strictly on the object. If the sensation of breath movement is present at the ânàpàna spot, the student knows this sensation. If there is no sensation of breath, the student continues to focus his or her attention on waiting for breath to cross the ânàpàna spot.

EFFORT

When the meditator initially starts the Ânàpànàsati practice, the physical and mental energy need to be high. Cultivating a positive attitude when beginning this practice is very useful. If the energy is allowed to wane too early in the practice, there is insufficient energy to sustain the attention at the ânàpàna spot long enough to cultivate the jhâna factors.

A metaphor that Ven. Pa Auk Sayadaw approved was of running downhill. Imagine you need to run down a long hill to meet someone at the bottom. You would initially begin to run as hard and fast as you could. However, once your physical momentum reached enough downhill force, you would lessen your physical effort and allow gravity to begin to carry you. The rest of the downhill run would be best accomplished by maintaining a vigilant balance between your effort and relaxing to let gravity work. The faster you are moving and the steeper the hill, the less personal effort you need to maintain.

Ânàpànàsati Meditation is much like this. As the jhâna factors begin to arise, extinguishing the hindrances, less effort is required to maintain attention on the breath at the ânàpàna spot. As the jhâna factors are first beginning to arise, you need to maintain a good amount of personal effort. After a while the meditator can begin to *slightly* lessen his or her personal effort. If the jhâna factors are stabilizing, the reduction in effort does not lessen the jhâna factors' intensity. There begins a delicate balance between lessening the personal effort and allowing the jhâna factors to begin to strengthen in their own time. This also reflects a thinning of the personal will or the sense of "me," which becomes more important in progressing through the jhânas.

We cannot stress the importance of a vigorous initial effort and a deliberate lessening of effort—an allowing—once the jhâna factors gain sufficient strength. One could also think of this as "relaxing" into the jhâna or "surrendering" to the jhâna. To enter jhâna, the practice takes over control. As the jhâna factors increase, they take over the primary work of concentrating on their own. Personal effort can diminish naturally. This is very difficult to communicate. We do not want to encourage meditators to lessen up on their effort too soon. Doing so dissipates the concentration that is building by practicing wholesomeness and uninterruptedly maintaining the attention at the ânàpàna spot. If, on the other hand, the personal effort is not reduced *at the right time*, the power generated by the jhâna factors does not take over and allow the nimitta to appear and stabilize.

PUTTING ASIDE WHAT WE KNOW

Virtually everyone undertaking jhâna practice has prior experience with one or more types of meditation. While learning these practices, however, the retreatant *must* disregard each and every other type of meditation known.

For example, the retreat we attended with Ven. Pa Auk Sayadaw included many students who were quite skilled in the Vipassana mindfulness meditation that is taught in the West in the lineage of Ven. Mahasi Sayadaw. We witnessed that upon arising from seated meditation, many fellow retreatants began the well-known "mindful walking" meditation. Also during public question sessions, there were many questions regarding how to "be mindful" while doing walking meditation. Often the teachers responded to the effect that it was good to "be mindful" while walking. Regrettably, the retreat leaders and retreatants were unaware that they were not talking the same language of meditation. They were using the word "mindful" differently. In the Ânàpànàsati Meditation practice, the word mindful *always* means placing and sustaining attention on the breath as it crosses the ânàpàna spot, no matter what you are doing. Because of this confusion, in our opinion, the retreatants released much of the concentrated meditative energy accumulated during meditation by shifting to another meditation object (i.e., the mindfulness of their walking).

Students must also put aside what they know of other methods of jhâna practice taught in the West. Other methods are different, and if a student applies those approaches, he or she may lose the concentration gained and prevent full absorption into the jhânas from arising. For example, switching the meditative object from the breath crossing the ânàpàna spot to a jhâna factor will immediately begin to disperse the level of concentration. It will feel pleasant but will gradually erode the ability to move from access concentration into absorption, possibly without the meditator even knowing that is happening.

Ânàpànàsati Meditation, in a jhâna retreat, is done to the *absolute exclusion* of everything else. Imagine that you are having a multi-course meal at a fine restaurant. Your task is to consume the meal while searching exclusively for the taste of salt. You do not want to taste anything but salt. In each bite you want to find salt. Salt, salt, salt—nothing else is tasted. This is the kind of focus to apply at the ânàpàna spot while undertaking any activity on a jhâna retreat.

THE USE OF RESOLVES

Resolving to stay in jhâna for a specific duration and emerging from jhâna at a determined time are two of the five jhâna masteries Ven. Pa Auk Sayadaw teaches. The use of resolves is a meditative skill that one is expected to develop. For example, a time resolve such as, "May first jhâna arise for three hours" is typical of what we used on the retreat with Ven. Pa Auk Sayadaw.

We also incorporated the use of other resolves in order to cultivate specific jhâna factors and/or absorption into a particular jhâna. The form Tina used was to very subtly "resolve" for a jhâna factor or a specific jhâna to arise by silently saying a phrase such as, "May piti increase strongly" or "May the first jhâna arise strongly" before a meditation period. Then she would let go of the thought or intention and settle back on the breath crossing the ânàpàna spot. This only takes a few seconds, so as not to dissipate concentration. A resolve is not a mantra or grasping statement. It is not repeated over and over. It is simply a single resolution to open to the arising of a particular aspect of practice.

In Stephen's use of resolves early in the jhâna retreat and prior to settling into the Ânàpànàsati Meditation, he would silently say to himself, "There is no identity in these thoughts; there is no identity in these emotions; there is no identity in these memories;

there is no identity in this body; there is no identity in these feelings; there is no identity in these perceptions." He called these "anatta/no-self resolves." This was helpful to his jhâna practice, as it thinned the normal sense of identity to better allow the jhânas to arise. If some other topic arose to be included, he would do so. And, he used the regular jhâna factor and jhâna resolves as well. He also found a silent offering of daily gratitude and appreciation for the Ânàpànàsati Meditation and its progression deepened the intimacy of the meditation.

After the first day or two, the resolves would arise quickly and pass through awareness as an expression of meditative intention. A little later in the retreat, there would be an energetic experience of these resolves without needing to have the resolve expressed internally with words. At the appropriate time, we would open to the energy of these now unspoken resolves. (As the meditator moves to various jhânas or practices, the resolve changes appropriately.)

MEDITATION TIMING

We highly recommend that meditators intending to participate in a jhâna retreat begin to meditate longer and longer periods of time prior to the retreat. If you are comfortable meditating for forty minutes once a day, increase to forty minutes two or three times a day. As that becomes comfortable, increase each period to one hour per meditation period. If your preparation period allows, we suggest getting to the point where you can meditate two hours twice a day. This gives you a very good start. If you are able to begin the Ânàpànàsati practice a week or two prior to the commencement of the retreat, this assists your progress also.

Once the retreat begins, meditate as long and as often as you can. Ideally you want to be meditating three to four periods a day. If possible, within the first week or ten days each time period should be increased to one, two, then three hours. "Two hours is better than one hour, and three hours is better than two hours," was Ven. Pa Auk Sayadaw's direction.

Many people think this is impossible to do. This is where it is very important to understand the difference between practices that cultivate momentary concentration and practices that cultivate deep access concentration and eventual absorption into the jhânas. At the time of the Pa Auk retreat, both of us had previously done extensive other practices that cultivate momentary concentration, such as Mahasi-style Vipassana mindfulness, the Tibetan Dzogchen practice of rigpa, and shikantaza meditation practice of Zen. While it was possible for us to meditate for several consecutive hours doing these practices on previous long retreats, we reflected that it was much more of a struggle to do those practices for many hours than it was to do jhâna meditation.

When Ven. Pa Auk Sayadaw told Tina to do three hours and eventually four hours in the first jhâna, she told him she thought she couldn't do it. She had never meditated that long before. But because in the jhânas the hindrances have dropped—completely in some cases—it is possible to feel pleasant and not in pain while one is meditating for a long time. And, when the awareness is absorbed fully into a jhâna, it is most definitely possible because most outer distractions are not perceived with the senses or are so slight that they don't matter. Even at the Pa Auk retreat, when we tried to sit for hours listening to a dharma talk, we found the experience different and more difficult than sitting for hours in deep access or absorption concentration. This demonstrates the contrast between strong and weak concentration. The relief from the hindrances, and the blissful feelings of the jhâna factors present with strong concentration, are what make it possible to sit for long hours.

In addition, because Westerners have not been raised for their entire lives to sit on zafus on the floor like Asians traditionally have, the Ven. Pa Auk Sayadaw graciously allows people to use a chair when necessary and when doing multi-hour sitting periods. He does prefer that students use the traditional floor posture, and in fact, on our retreat there were several Asian retreatants who sat only on a grass mat with no cushion! But, for Westerners, the Ven. Pa Auk Sayadaw feels it is most important to do what best facilitates effective practice. So, use a chair if necessary, maintaining effective, upright posture with your feet on the floor.

To cultivate both your ability *and* your *belief* that two or three hours of continuous meditation is possible, when you do formal meditation, sit for the *entire time period* you intended before the meditation began. If you told yourself you would meditate for an hour, do not arise until an hour has passed. If two hours, sit for two hours. You need to develop the time commitment discipline very early on the jhâna retreat. With the bliss of the jhâna factors, this is not only possible but also enjoyable. After two weeks, you should be able to meditate for the entire time period without moving or moving very little. This may sound difficult to downright impossible, but it isn't. It is a matter of opening yourself to the reality that tens of thousands of meditators throughout history have been able to do this. If you are convinced you can do it, you will be amazed to learn you can.

"PSYCHIC POWERS"

As we detail the many practices we learned from Ven. Pa Auk Sayadaw, some people may be surprised to see these types of practices as part of a traditional Buddhist path, or they may think "psychic powers" are required to complete them. However, using powers beyond normal awareness is a time-honored practice, known throughout Buddhism for more than twenty-five hundred years, starting with the Buddha. We also have precedents of modern teachers such as Ven. Pa Auk Sayadaw and Dipa Ma, not to mention the many lay and monastic practitioners at Pa Auk Monastery in Myanmar (Burma) who do these practices daily.

To provide another context, in the *Samannaphala Sutta, DN 2,* the Buddha directs that "the mind thus concentrated, purified, and bright, unblemished, free from defects, pliant, malleable, steady, and attained to imperturbability, is directed and inclined to the modes of supranormal powers." It is worth noting that the Buddha does *not* say supernatural, *rather* supranormal. These powers are not outside, or beyond, what is natural. Rather, the meditative powers or abilities used in Buddhist practice are merely beyond what is considered normal.

As the mind is collected, unified, and stable through the rise of the jhâna factors and entry into absorption, a purified brightness of mind is apparent. This laser-like concentration is focused and capable of penetrating in a nonordinary manner. It is sometimes referred to as the "divine eye" or "wisdom eye." (See *Ariyapariyesana Sutta MN26.)* The wisdom eye is used to some extent in nearly all of the meditations used in this book, including the Ânàpànàsati Meditation, Thirty-Two Body Parts Meditation, Skeleton Meditation, Kasina Meditations, Sublime Abiding Meditations, Protective Meditations, and Four Elements Meditation.

While modern practitioners may see these practices as beyond what is normally possible, we encourage you to remember that thousands of Buddhists have done these practices for more than twenty-five hundred years. The Buddha identified doubt as one of the five hindrances. Your own confidence and lack of doubt will serve you well as you undertake these practices.

TYPES OF CONCENTRATION:
MOMENTARY, ACCESS, AND ABSORPTION

Meditators will encounter all three types of concentration in this practice. It is important to understand what they are, how they are different, and how they fit together. *Momentary* concentration is the most difficult to understand conceptually, because there are two types.

The first type of momentary concentration develops in Vipassana insight practices in which the object changes frequently. In contrast to meditation practices in which the object is stable or fairly continuous, in this type of momentary concentration the object is, in a way, "moving." As such, one could say that the ultimate object of these practices is the present moment and what is being perceived in the present moment.

Insight-oriented momentary concentration practices are widely used in the West and can be found in meditation such as Mahasi-style mindfulness, Tibetan Dzogchen rigpa, and the shikantaza meditation practice of Zen. Ven. Pa Auk Sayadaw teaches the Four Elements Meditation as the entry point into the Vipassana practices. The Four Elements meditation is a momentary concentration practice.

The second type of momentary concentration is used for Samatha practices. In this case, the object is more stable, which leads to serenity and purification of mind. Ven. Pa Auk Sayadaw also refers to this type of momentary concentration as "preparatory" concentration, because it prepares the meditator for and precedes access concentration. In the Samatha practice leading to jhâna, the meditator takes the natural breath and eventually the smoke or white-colored nimitta is the initial object. To distinguish momentary from access concentration, one could say that the object is not yet energized at the higher level of access concentration.

Meditators can eventually attain *access concentration* using either type of momentary concentration practice—Samatha or Vipassana. However, Samatha practices are more likely to lead to access concentration because of their more stable nature. Access concentration is characterized by the reduction or complete dropping of the five hindrances and the arising and strengthening of the jhâna factors. In access concentration, the meditative experience becomes smoother, easier, and more pleasant because of this dropping of hindrances and the arising of the powerful and blissful sensations of the jhâna factors. This allows the practitioner to meditate longer and progress more easily in the practice. One could say that it becomes a positive, self-reinforcing loop. In access concentration, in the Samatha practice of jhâna, the transparent and bright nimitta merged with the breath (the ânàpàna nimitta) becomes the object.

Most of the practices outlined in this book are Samatha practices specifically designed to settle the mind and develop laser-like awareness, leading eventually to full absorption into the jhânas. In access concentration, the jhâna factors are present but insufficiently strong for full absorption into jhâna. With progression to each successive jhâna, one will first experience access concentration as the awareness orients to the new experiences and increases in stability.

Examples of Samatha practices designed to develop access and absorption concentration are Ânàpànàsati Meditation (as taught by Ven. Pa Auk Sayadaw), the Kasinas, Thirty-Two Body Parts, Skeleton, and the Bramaviharas/Sublime Abidings.

Some people are attracted to practices that cultivate deep concentration because of the extremely blissful sensations of the jhâna factors that begin in access concentration. This can be both a blessing and a curse. As a blessing, it attracts one to nonordinary experiences and allows one to meditate longer and more intently, with little awareness of physical pain or outside distractions. As a curse, it can become a trap, because the practice cannot progress to absorption if there is attachment to focusing on the jhāna factors just to experience bliss. And, as one progresses through the jhānas, one must be willing to let a particular jhāna factor drop in order to move on.

The word "jhāna" means absorption, so the two words are synonymous. In *absorption concentration,* awareness is pulled into the jhāna with a "snap." The beginning meditator cannot "will" the absorption to happen or "make" it happen. It only happens when the concentration is strong and ripe after many hours, days, or weeks of unwavering focus on a specific meditative object. Only later, as one becomes more skilled with the progression of jhānas and the five jhāna masteries, is it possible to enter a jhāna at will.

In absorption, in addition to the extremely strong presence of the appropriate jhāna factors, the awareness is extremely secluded and focused, and ongoing concentration is more easily maintained. Awareness fully penetrates and is suffused by the jhāna factors. The *Visuddhimagga* highlights the difference between access and absorption concentration using the analogy of walking. Access concentration is like a young child learning to walk. It can walk a few steps but repeatedly falls down. In contrast, absorption concentration is like an adult who is able to stand and walk for an entire day without falling down (*Visuddimagga,* IV, 33, p. 125). A modern Western metaphor would be of a top spinning. In access concentration, the top needs constant attention, wobbles frequently, and falls down. In absorption, the top spins in a centered and focused way on its own.

There may be misconceptions about the experience of full absorption in jhāna. Firstly, there *is* awareness while in jhāna.

It is not a zombie state, trance, or unconscious period of time. The only awareness while in full absorption is of the object. If the meditator has awareness of data from the five senses, it is because he or she is temporarily out of absorption jhâna. The five sense doors (sight, hearing, touch, taste, and smell) do not arise while in absorption jhâna. This is why the meditator must make a resolve on when to emerge from jhâna beforehand, because there is no decision-making or thought while fully absorbed in jhâna. Beginning jhâna practitioners who find themselves thinking or noticing the input from the sense doors should view this as a slight imperfection of jhâna, not jhâna itself. One can also "pop out" of jhâna unintentionally because concentration wanes. In fact, this happens frequently, which can be frustrating if it happens before the time requirement for jhâna mastery is fulfilled. It is best not to worry about initial imperfections as these are bound to happen as the beginner is developing jhâna mastery. As concentration increases, these imperfections wane and stability increases.

Awareness in the jhânas is incredibly pristine, purifying, and indescribable. It is distinctly different from access concentration. However, because access concentration can be so pleasant and nonordinary, it is easy to believe that access concentration is actually absorption, when it is not. This is why it is important to receive guidance from a qualified teacher who knows the difference between access concentration and absorption concentration. (See the *Visuddhimagga*, 5th ed., page 99, paragraph 64.)

Absorption concentration is an incredibly powerful tool for purification, refinement of awareness, and access to realms far beyond normal, everyday comprehension. In addition, this laser-like focus can be an incredibly powerful tool to carry into the Vipassana insight practice. Meditation powered by the super-charged energy of the jhânas, or access concentration, can provide access to insight that may not be possible with momentary concentration alone.

Because the practitioner's awareness is so refined in doing this practice, sensory input that would seem minimal in ordinary consciousness can feel extremely jarring to the practitioner when emerging from jhâna and upon having completed weeks or months of deep absorption practice and re-entering worldly life.

NIMITTA

Nimitta is a very important component of this practice. At its most simple, it is a sign of powerful concentration. Nimitta arises in access concentration as a sign that the mind is unifying. One can find references of it in descriptions of modern meditation teachers such as Dipa Ma, who describes a light when she meditates, even during mindfulness practice.

The nimitta is light seen visually in the mind's eye. It is not a light seen with the eyes. The nimitta arises on its own as a product of the natural unification of mind that develops with concentration. At first, we cannot will it to arise or make it arise. (Later, as mastery increases, the nimitta arises at will as do the jhânas.)

The nimitta usually starts as a faint flickering of light. It may also start as a smoky experience of the breath, like exhaling in cold winter temperatures. For others, it may appear as a round light, similar to a train headlight. The nimitta can appear as a variety of colors and shapes. Sometimes the nimitta appears at a distance from the meditator. Do not give any significance to the nimitta features.

Whatever the nimitta looks like or does, at this point the meditator does *not* focus on it or look directly at it. The breath crossing the ânàpànà spot continues to be the meditation object. As enticing as it is, don't even glance at the nimitta. Almost everyone, despite explicit instruction, tries to look at or move their attention toward the nimitta. When we do this, the nimitta usually fades or disappears. It's similar to trying to grab a cloud in your clenched fist. No matter how strong the desire to hold the cloud, it always remains out of reach. So, at this point, the student's attention stays on the breath crossing the ânàpànà spot despite any excitement or desire to go to the nimitta.

When the meditator stays with the breath crossing the ânàpànà spot and *does not chase* the nimitta, the nimitta moves closer to the ânàpànà spot. Without using any effort, the nimitta and the breath at the ânàpànà spot move closer and closer. As they move closer together, the student stays with the breath crossing the ânàpànà spot until the nimitta merges *by itself* with the breath at the ânàpànà spot. When the meditator stays with the breath at the ânàpànà spot and *does not chase* the nimitta, the two *will* eventually merge together.

This merging of the nimitta with the breath happens *only* when the time is ripe. It is like trying to pet a very shy animal. If you pursue the animal, it flees. However, if you wait a safe distance from the animal, in its own time, it comes to you.

When ripe, the attention shifts in a snap, *by itself*, and the breath crossing the ânàpànà spot and the nimitta merge into one. We cannot say how this happens, but it does. Once the ânàpànà spot merges with the nimitta, you then have the "nimitta/ânàpànà spot" combination as your object. (We will refer to this throughout the remainder of the book as the ânàpànà nimitta.) This is a new phase of practice and a very exciting one!

The ânàpànà nimitta eventually becomes very stable. Each time you close your eyes, the ânàpànà nimitta is present. The meditator, meditating with ânàpànà nimitta as the object, restricts all outflows of attention and energy. It's best to keep the eyes downcast, movements measured, and stay away from any inner or outer talking. The ânàpànà nimitta expands if the meditator is patient. If the meditator attempts to expand the ânàpànà nimitta before the concentration is developed sufficiently, it breaks apart, fades, or disappears. If this happens, return the attention to the breath crossing the ânàpànà spot and wait for nimitta to again arise and merge.

We both had the ânàpànà nimitta break or fade on us several times, as we were initially too excited to wait for it to intensify and expand on its own. For some people, during this phase the ânàpànà nimitta envelops the entire body. If this happens, let it do so; just make sure you can still see it also. Over time, the ânàpànà nimitta stabilizes. Again, surrender your personal effort to the experience and allow the ânàpànà nimitta to move and change as it wishes. It is common here for the meditator to feel excitement, sometimes wondering whether this is the first jhâna. As this is a progression, you can expect to have a fair amount of time with the ânàpànà nimitta in access concentration before the first jhâna arises. Just remain in silence internally.

"Sinking mind" can be a problem at this point in the process. This happens when the meditator's concentration exceeds his or her energy in the body. Because one is sitting so still for so many hours a day, and the experience of "effort" has lessened as concentration has increased, this is a delicate time in which balance is helpful. It is okay to walk at a pace in which the physical energy can be elevated (rather than the very slow mindful walking done in the Mahasi-style mindfulness practice). Just make sure that you maintain your focus on the ânàpànà nimitta the entire time you are walking with eyes open.

Ven. Pa Auk Sayadaw encourages students to maintain meditative stability on the ânàpànà nimitta continuously for a minimum of thirty minutes (the longer you maintain it, the more stable and focused the concentration is) and then make a resolve to enter first jhâna. If the resolve feels like a distraction and you do not want to use one, you can just wait until concentration is strong enough and the jhâna may arise on its own. Regardless of whether or not one makes a resolve, only when concentration is strong enough will awareness be drawn into the first jhâna. It feels as though the ânàpànà nimitta physically "grabs you by the lapels and pulls you face first" into the absorption. It is very distinct and unmistakable, different from access concentration. If you resolve to enter first jhâna over and over before the time is ripe, your concentration will wane, and you will remain in access concentration. While access concentration is very pleasant and all the jhâna factors are present, it is not full absorption into a jhâna.

In this chapter, we have discussed a solid foundation upon which the jhâna practice can be built. From the appearance and stabilization of the ânàpànà nimitta, the meditator is close to being drawn into the full jhâna absorption. We will next present the four form jhânas, including all kasinas used to complete the practice of the lower jhânas.

CHAPTER 3

FORM JHÂNAS
(ONE THROUGH FOUR)
AND RELATED PRACTICES

We will now explore the four form jhânas, jhâna mastery, Thirty-Two Body Parts Meditation, Skeleton Meditation, and each of the kasinas used with the four form jhânas. Specifically, we will discuss what we believe are the best methods for practicing these meditations to the point of mastery.

ABSORPTION—FIRST JHÂNA

Jhâna only appears when the conditions for it are ripe. A beginning jhâna practitioner cannot force the awareness into full absorption or make it happen. The student must be vigilant *while relaxing* into the process. The meditator is either pulled into the jhâna spontaneously or uses a resolve for the first time entering a jhâna. Do not become discouraged as you focus on the ânâpânà nimitta, allowing concentration to build, but also do not become overly zealous and use the resolves repeatedly to the point that your concentration wanes.

"You," as you usually know yourself, do *not* enter jhâna.

Rather, the veils layered and known as the "normal you" have been temporarily peeling away in the Ânàpànàsati Meditation. A thinner, gauzelike sense of self is what merges/absorbs in jhâna. There is an awareness of being in jhâna while in jhâna. It is *not* an unconscious state. One is aware only of the meditation object. In full absorption, there is no awareness of time, the body, or the physical senses. However, due to the deep concentration, the beginning meditator's mind may be able to quickly shift from absorption to access concentration. Fortunately, it is also possible to quickly shift back into jhâna absorption knowing this to be a slight imperfection of jhâna. In this case, the meditator may have a slight sense of time, the body, or physical senses. As the practice matures, this sense will drop and awareness will be only of the object.

The meditator remains absorbed until the jhâna factors weaken or the time resolve ends. After jhâna has ended, there remains a deeply felt peace. It is our belief that the purified personal sense of consciousness merges into unobstructed, impersonal consciousness. The process of jhâna feels as though an ongoing purification has occurred. Each meditative period in jhâna seems to unify the mind, removing further impurities.

We will not be describing the actual experience of any jhâna. There are two reasons why: First, there may be a tendency for meditators using this writing as a guide to try and duplicate what we experienced. Second, each meditator's localized consciousness is slightly different. As this localized consciousness enters jhâna and is purified through jhâna, the experience is unique for each person.

STABILITY

Great contentment accompanies meditative stability. Ven. Pa Auk Sayadaw requires his students to remain fully absorbed in various jhânas for three or occasionally even four hours before declaring that they have completed this phase and have gained mastery. To the thinking mind, a few hours of meditation sounds challenging but possible. In first jhâna, however, the awareness is so close to normal consciousness that it is quite easy for full absorption to be disrupted. If you are required to stay absorbed in jhâna for three hours to achieve jhâna mastery and you pop out of jhâna after two hours and fifty minutes, that period was insufficient for mastery. Also, if while in jhâna you notice the thinking mind making comments, you are out of jhâna. You then begin again in your next meditation period. Accordingly, you can expect to do countless meditation periods with first jhâna before this time requirement is satisfied. This allows a confidence and familiar stability with each jhâna to develop.

Ven. Pa Auk Sayadaw requires his students to stay in the first jhâna, completing two to three hours per sitting for a minimum of three days, as well as having the jhâna be instantly accessible, before moving on to the second jhâna. This is because each jhâna must be stable before moving on or concentration wanes and is difficult to recover. Subsequent to the first jhâna and for all of the kasinas, Ven. Pa Auk Sayadaw requires the meditator to be absorbed in each jhâna for a minimum of one meditation period of three hours.

The student goes through the first and all subsequent jhânas each and every time a higher jhâna is sought. For example, if the student is approaching third jhâna for the first time, the student enters first jhâna for a brief period, enters second jhâna for a brief period, and then opens toward third jhâna. The student never goes straight into third jhâna without going through first and second jhâna, respectively.

While there can be some anticipation about the subsequent

jhâna, unless you have strong stability in first jhâna, you can not enter second jhâna. If a student tries to enter second jhâna too soon, both the first and second jhâna may fade. The student then needs to return to breath as it crosses the ânàpàna spot to develop stability with the ânàpàna nimitta before the first jhâna arises again. The jhânas are a purification of consciousness. Each level of purification is needed at each jhâna before the meditator is ready for the next jhâna. As each jhâna is mastered, there is an inclination toward the next higher jhâna. Ironically, the jhâna factors that are unnecessary for the next jhâna begin to feel coarse and burdensome, like carrying too many pieces of luggage on a trip. Most students are likely to feel satisfied releasing the jhâna factors that are no longer needed for the next higher jhâna.

THE FOUR FORM JHÂNAS AND ASSOCIATED JHÂNA FACTORS

With each progressive jhâna, various factors drop as the mind purifies and awareness becomes more focused and concentrated. The progression is as follows:

- First Jhâna—vitakka, vicâra, piti, sukha, and ekaggatâ
- Second Jhâna—piti, sukha, and ekaggatâ
- Third Jhâna—sukha and ekaggatâ
- Fourth Jhâna—ekaggatâ and upekkhâ

FIVE JHÂNA MASTERIES

Ven. Pa Auk Sayadaw requires students to gain the five masteries in the first jhâna before moving to the second jhâna. (*Visuddhimagga* IV, 131, p. 150.) Only when the teacher is satisfied that the student has indeed completed the five masteries in connection with the first jhâna (absorption), will the student be directed toward the second jhâna.

The five masteries are:

1. To advert (call or direct the attention to) the jhâna factors
2. To enter jhâna whenever desired
3. To resolve to stay in jhâna for a determined duration and to keep the time resolve
4. To emerge from jhâna at the determined time
5. To review the jhâna factors

While the first four are self-explanatory, the fifth mastery requires further explanation. This will be discussed below in the bhavanga section.

BHAVANGA (BHAVAÏGA)

Of all the topics covered here, this is the topic we least understand conceptually. We are not Buddhist scholars. We are unable to explain anything about bhavanga except how it is used in jhâna practice.

The bhavanga is located in the heart region. It is luminous and transparent like a mirror. Ven. Pa Auk Sayadaw instructs that, according to the Suttanta Method, it is also metaphorically called the "mind-door" because mind-door cognitive processes such as jhâna cognitive processes, including the jhâna factors, arise depending on it. When a meditator reflects upon jhâna factors she or he must first discern that bhavanga-mind-door. When jhâna objects, such as ânàpànà nimitta, appear in that mind-door, she or he can see jhâna factors in it because jhâna factors arise depending on the mind-door.

The student examines the bhavanga with the wisdom eye either before entering the second or higher jhâna or after exiting jhâna to determine which jhâna factors are, or were, present. Somehow, following the time when the student enters first jhâna, the ability to discern the jhâna factors in the bhavanga comes naturally. We personally had no idea how this would occur when we first heard about it at the retreat. We thought it might be impossible to see into the bhavanga with the wisdom eye. Yet with the wisdom eye functioning, seeing the jhâna factors in the bhavanga is possible.

The instruction when exiting a jhâna meditation is for the student to look very briefly with the wisdom eye to determine if he or she can see into the bhavanga. After the next sitting, at its end, the meditator checks briefly whether he or she can see *each* of the five jhâna factors (vitakka, vicâra, piti, sukha, and ekaggatâ) in the bhavanga. Only at this time does the student attempt the remaining four masteries. At the *end* of *that* sitting, the meditator again checks the bhavanga to see whether the five jhâna factors were present. At a later sitting, the meditator attempts all five masteries and then checks all five jhâna factors *at once, as a unified whole.*

In all these cases, the student is *not* looking with the normal eye(s) toward the heart area to see bhavanga. The wisdom eye develops through the purification process of Ânàpànàsati Meditation and jhâna. The wisdom eye becomes quite powerful as a result of the bright jhâna energy. Reviewing the jhâna factors in the bhavanga is required to master each of the subsequent jhânas as well. Rest assured, upon completing first jhâna, you will be able to discern the jhâna factors in bhavanga.

SECOND JHÂNA

Following the student's attaining the five jhâna masteries in the first jhâna, the teacher instructs the student to proceed to second jhâna. We found, having attained the five masteries of first jhâna, that we were instinctively oriented toward second jhâna.

The second jhâna does not have vitakka or vicâra as its jhâna factors. The second jhâna has piti, sukha, and ekaggatâ as its jhâna factors.

The meditator returns to the ânàpànà nimitta in meditation. If the nimitta is not present, the meditator continues focusing on the breath crossing the ânàpànà spot until nimitta again arises. Usually if you have entered first jhâna, the nimitta is readily available, presuming outer and inner talk remain silent and the attention on the object is ongoing. Shortly after starting with the attention on the breath crossing the ânàpànà spot, the nimitta appears strong and clearly present. The student then cultivates the first five jhâna factors (vitakka, vicâra, piti, sukha, and ekaggatâ) and enters first jhâna. The beginning student always enters first jhâna before proceeding to second jhâna. At no time does the student jump over any jhâna (meaning you do not start with third jhâna without having proceeded through first jhâna and second jhâna). On the first attempt, do first jhâna for an extended period until it is stable, and then make a resolve for second jhâna. Later, the meditator can spend only a few minutes in first jhâna and then go on to the second jhâna.

Entering the second jhâna, the two jhâna factors of first jhâna (vitakka and vicâra) drop away. The unnecessary jhâna factors for successively higher jhânas drop upon entering the higher jhâna. Again, when ready, a resolve is made and, if concentration is strong and the time is ripe, awareness is drawn into second jhâna.

Interestingly, each jhâna has a different feel, flavor, or intuitive taste than the other jhânas. With time and experience you may learn to experientially distinguish which jhâna is present. The student will quickly review the bhavanga after exiting jhâna to determine which jhâna factors were present in that jhâna. This confirms which jhâna has been entered.

Again, Ven. Pa Auk Sayadaw requires jhâna mastery of the second jhâna. This means the student spends three continuous hours in the second jhâna during one period of meditation. In other words, the student cannot be in second jhâna one meditation period for one hour, in second jhâna during another meditation period for two hours and add them together to have that satisfy the mastery requirement. Jhâna stability, meaning fulfilling the five jhâna masteries, is required to fully experience each jhâna and to have the purification and jhâna energy to proceed with stability to the next higher jhâna. Once the five jhâna masteries are achieved in the second jhâna, the student is directed to the third jhâna.

THIRD JHÂNA

This jhâna has only sukha and ekaggatâ as its jhâna factors. The meditator continues focusing on the ânàpànà nimitta. If nimitta is not available, the student focuses on the breath crossing the ânàpànà spot until the nimitta appears and merges with the spot. The student proceeds to once again enter and exit the first and second jhâna as before. The time spent in the first and second jhânas is brief. As soon as the student feels the stability and bright, clear energy of the first jhâna, he or she exits the first jhâna. Upon entering second absorption jhâna, vitakka and vicâra drop, as they are unnecessary for second jhâna.

Piti is a mental state that produces a corresponding body sensation of happiness, almost an excitement. As before when opening to third jhâna, the jhâna factors of second jhâna feel unnecessary, almost a burden. Sukha as a deep feeling of bliss is very appropriate when developing the third jhâna factors. Ekaggatâ is unified, focused awareness. The meditative attention and awareness unify. There is really no extra effort exerted by the student. The nimitta draws the student into third jhâna with the jhâna factors of sukha and ekaggatâ. The third jhâna feels more refined and pure than the second jhâna.

Each successively higher jhâna is easier to maintain, as it is further from ordinary consciousness, so the senses are less easily distracted. We found each jhâna to be independently wonderful. Each jhâna was very satisfying. Yet once the five jhâna masteries were achieved, there was an obvious movement, almost attraction, toward the next higher jhâna. Once the five jhâna masteries have been reached with the third jhâna, the student proceeds to fourth jhâna. The student begins by discarding, turning away from, sukha as no longer necessary for the fourth jhâna. Sukha is replaced from the fourth jhâna through the four formless jhânas by *upekkhâ* (equanimity). Or, as concentration focuses into one-pointedness and equanimity, sukha can begin to wane on its own.

FOURTH JHÂNA

Fourth jhâna has ekaggatâ (one-pointedness) and upekkhâ (equanimity) as its jhâna factors. Upekkhâ replaces sukha as a more refined and less gross mentally produced feeling state, which will be present throughout the rest of the jhânas. The student focuses on the ânâpânâ nimitta and enters first jhâna with its five jhâna factors (vitakka, vicâra, piti, sukha, and ekaggatâ). After a few minutes in the stability of first jhâna, first jhâna is exited, and the student enters second jhâna through the nimitta, with the factors of second jhâna (piti, sukha, and ekaggatâ). When stability in the second jhâna is reached for a few minutes, the student exits the second jhâna and uses the nimitta to enter third jhâna. The third jhâna factors (sukha and ekaggatâ) are present prior to entering third jhâna. The first time attempting fourth jhâna, the meditator may stay in third jhâna for an extended period to ensure stability. Over time, a brief stay is all that is needed to confirm the stability and energy of the third jhâna, as with the prior two jhânas. The student exits the third jhâna and feels the inclination toward ekaggatâ and upekkhâ.

Ekaggatâ and upekkhâ feel very full, grounded, and satisfying without having a quality of excitement as in the second and third jhâna. Stephen recalls anticipating that he would find the dropping of sukha to be difficult because of the pleasure of sukha. When the student is moving toward fourth jhâna, sukha feels unnecessary. The one-pointedness (ekaggatâ) and equanimity (upekkhâ) are very complete. It is very difficult to be distracted when the student is meditating with ekaggatâ and upekkhâ. There are almost no distractions to the meditator here.

When these two jhâna factors are strong and the nimitta is powerful, the meditator is drawn into fourth jhâna. The shift from third jhâna to fourth jhâna is significant. Moving from first jhâna to second jhâna or second jhâna to third jhâna is a slight change in jhâna factors. Experientially these first three form jhânas feel more similar to each other. The student must have the willingness to put down all the happy and blissful body sensations produced by the mental states of piti and sukha in the first three jhânas to focus on ekaggatâ and upekkhâ in the fourth jhâna. While some people may presume that fourth jhâna is more challenging because the bliss is much more subtle and impersonal, it was available by trusting the teachings and not just seeking pleasurable experiences. Being willing to develop ekaggatâ and upekkhâ to the exclusion of the other jhâna factors was natural after mastering third jhâna.

By the time the meditator is close to entering fourth jhâna, the normal breath has become very, very shallow and discrete. The *Visuddhimagga*, fifth edition, page 268, paragraph 179, states that the breath stops in the fourth jhâna. Experientially, it feels as though it has stopped. What is important is for the student not to be concerned about this issue. Any attention to whether there is, in fact, breath diverts the meditative concentration and fourth jhâna is not available. Specifically, there can be a bodily felt sense of fright when meditating with the nimitta as fourth jhâna ripens. This is because the body senses there is insufficient oxygen to live. Resist the urge to take a deep breath to pacify this fright. A deep breath at this time disrupts the development of ekaggatâ and upekkhâ and fourth jhâna becomes further away. Allow the fear of having insufficient breath to pass. The fear does, in fact, pass.

The meditator can check the jhâna factors in access concentration and make the resolve for fourth jhâna. Alternatively, when ripe, the concentration draws the awareness into fourth jhâna. The student proceeds as before to obtain five jhâna masteries for fourth jhâna.

FURTHER PRACTICES WITH THE FORM JHÂNAS

Once the first four jhânas are stable, the student and teacher may agree that the student should begin practice to enter the upper jhânas. In this case, the student does the following meditative practices in the following order:

- Thirty-Two Body Parts Meditation
- Skeleton Meditation
- White Kasina (all the kasina meditations are initially completed attaining the first through fourth jhâna using each progressive kasina as the object)
- Nila Kasina (brown/black/blue)
- Yellow Kasina
- Red Kasina
- Earth Kasina
- Water Kasina
- Fire Kasina

- Wind Kasina
- Light Kasina
- Space Kasina

We will now review the Thirty-Two Body Parts Meditation, Skeleton Meditation, and all Kasina Meditations through the fourth jhâna, in turn.

THIRTY-TWO BODY PARTS MEDITATION

Once the student has attained jhâna mastery of the fourth jhâna using Ânàpànàsati Meditation, the student is directed, by the teacher, to Thirty-Two Body Parts Meditation. This meditation is undertaken to loosen the student's identity with the body. This allows the student less attachment to the body as jhâna practice develops toward the upper formless jhânas. It also lays the foundation for nonattachment to the body in order to see the *rupa- kalàpas* later in the Vipassana practice. (Rupa-kalàpas are the basis of all materiality. They are described in the Four Elements Meditation chapter.)

The student is directed to again enter and pass through the first, second, third, and fourth jhânas using the ânàpànà nimitta as the object. Each of the four form jhânas is experienced with their corresponding jhâna factors. Jhâna mastery is obtained for each jhâna. The bhavanga is quickly checked after exiting each jhâna to ensure the correct jhâna factors were present in that particular jhâna. Each jhâna is exited only when the stability and jhâna energy are strongly experienced by the student. Typically this is completed in less than one meditation period. Once out of the fourth jhâna, the student directs the strong, clear, bright jhâna energy—the wisdom eye—to the body as follows. The body parts are listed below in groups, because at a later point the meditator discerns them together in these groups. Occasionally, when a student has strong paramis for this practice, it may be possible to discern all thirty-two body parts in one sitting.

Earth element parts:
- Body parts 1–5: head hairs, body hairs, nails, teeth, and skin
- Body parts 6–10: flesh, sinews, bones, bone marrow, and kidneys
- Body parts 11–15: heart, liver, membranes, spleen, and lungs
- Body parts 16–20: intestines, mesentery (this connects the small intestines to the abdominal wall), undigested food, feces, and brain

Water element parts:
- Body parts 1–6: bile, phlegm, pus, blood, sweat, and fat
- Body parts 7–12: tears, grease, saliva, snot, synovial fluid (this lubricates joints), and urine

Initially each part, such as head hairs, is located with the wisdom eye and observed internally. Each part is carefully examined and deeply known so that it can be experienced in the body in one instant. Should the brightness of jhâna energy fade during this practice, the student is directed back to the jhânas using the ânàpàna nimitta as the object, progressing through the first, second, third, and fourth jhâna for a meditation period to re-establish strong concentration. The student is then free to resume the Thirty-Two Body Parts Meditation.

Each body part should be seen very clearly. Characteristics such as the location, color and contour are known to the student before passing on to the next body part. The student discerns, for example, the blood everywhere in the body at once with eyes closed. The flow, pressure, and exact color of blood flowing within the body is experientially known to the student. The blood flowing is actually seen with the wisdom eye. Furthermore, this experience of blood is known every time blood is sought in this meditation. Once each Earth Element body part is easily locatable in the student's body, the student learns to see all five parts together *as a unit.* This is eventually completed for each group of body parts in the Earth Element and Water Element.

When the student can "see" with the jhâna energized wisdom eye all the elements of earth and water discretely and as a group, the student is directed to look at the Earth Element group, then the Water Element Group, as a whole. When the student has learned to do this quickly and thoroughly, the Earth Element and Water Element groups are seen together, with each element seen separately and as a unit of either Earth or Water, and as the whole of Thirty-Two Body Parts Meditation. This sounds impossible. Yet with the powerful, laser-like concentration functioning as the wisdom eye, it is possible for anyone to complete.

After all distinct body parts are exhaustively seen with the wisdom eye and can be experienced distinctly and together at once, the student is directed to begin to see each distinct body part in someone else, usually someone nearby in the meditation hall. Each distinct part is seen with the wisdom eye experientially in the other, sometimes with the eyes open and other times with the eyes shut. Once this has been done successfully, the student is directed to continue with *every* person, animal, or other being. Again, if the student begins to lag or lose energy while completing the Thirty-Two Body Parts Meditation, the student should go through the full four jhânas using the ânàpàna nimitta as the object before returning to the Thirty-Two Body Parts Meditation.

Eventually the student is able to discern every being (human, animal, or other) in all directions as the Thirty-Two Body Parts, Earth Element, and Water Element, and combined as one of Thirty-Two Body Parts Meditation. When this has been completed, the student is directed to Skeleton Meditation.

This may sound like it would take weeks or months to complete, but due to the strong jhâna energy, it took us about two days to complete. While the time it takes may vary from student to student, the point is that it moves quickly due to the laser-like clarity powered by the jhânas.

SKELETON MEDITATION

The student passes through the first, second, third, and fourth jhânas using the ânàpàna nimitta as the object, in preparation for Skeleton Meditation. This is done to maintain the brilliant, light, focused jhâna energy. The student next directs the wisdom eye to the bones of her or his own skeleton. Since seeing one's own skeleton was accomplished previously as part of the Thirty-Two Body Parts Meditation, returning to this practice is fairly effortless. The skeleton is seen as a whole. Color variations, breaks, or cracks in the bones can be seen. The meditator holds this sight with the wisdom eye during meditation. After the skeleton is seen in its entirety in one instant, the student is instructed by the teacher to develop a feeling of repulsiveness for the skeleton.

Repulsiveness (patikula or asubha) is used in various meditations to loosen the identity with your body. This loosening of the identification with the body is helpful to successfully enter the kasinas and upper formless jhânas. Thus the student develops this repulsiveness toward her or his own body. The meditator is encouraged to see with the wisdom eye the frailties of the skeleton.

As the development of repulsiveness for the skeleton strengthens with jhâna energy, the mental image of skeleton eventually ceases and the skeleton as a physical identity drops away. The sense of repulsiveness of the skeleton remains as a meditative object.

As the strength of this repulsive meditation develops, it is possible to have first jhâna arise using the repulsiveness of the skeleton as the meditative object. In any event, the student is instructed to exhaustively see the "skeleton as repulsive" in his or her own body. When successful, the student is directed to see the "skeleton as repulsive" in another person. Seeing others as their skeleton is completed with eyes closed. This is repeated with others until the student can quickly move their attention from person to person and see only repulsiveness for the skeleton. Once this is satisfactorily accomplished, the student is directed to see the "skeleton as repulsive" in every body in all directions throughout the world. The student needs to see the skeleton clearly in this meditation, as this can be the entry for white kasina later. Also, this meditation helps the student to relax his or her identity with their physical body. In the upper formless jhânas, the personal consciousness localized in the student must be free to merge/ absorb into the more impersonal consciousnesses of each upper jhâna. Once Skeleton Meditation is completed, the student is ready for White Kasina practice.

KASINAS (KASIÕA)

Kasinas are seen as disc-like objects of various colors or elements. The jhânas entered using the different kasinas each have a distinct flavor of experience. There are also, of course, similarities. Progressing through the kasinas in the following order allows a thinning and purifying of the meditator's consciousness. The kasinas are undertaken in this specific order, because each progressive kasina is more refined and insubstantial as a meditative object. This prepares the student for the subtle objects of meditation in the upper formless jhânas. Also, the meditator's awareness with each subsequent kasina becomes more purified, more refined, and less dense. This is preparing the student for entering the formless jhânas.

Finding the proper color for the color kasinas can be tricky. The student can use the various colors in the body as witnessed in the Thirty-Two Body Parts Meditation. Using one's own body parts is the traditional instruction. In the old days, this undoubtedly made the practice easier because the color was always available to the meditator. However, if the student prefers, the colors of nature such as flowers, soil, trees, clouds, and so on can be used. In either case, the optimal color has been located when the student shuts his or her eyes and the color can be seen clearly and distinctly in the mind's eye. Alternately, if using an object in nature, the color is first observed with eyes open. When the student can see the color very clearly with the eyes shut, the color kasina meditation can commence for that specific color.

MEDITATIVE PROCEDURE FOR EACH KASINA IN THE FORM JHÂNAS (ONE THROUGH FOUR)

The process is the same for each kasina through the first, second, third, and fourth jhâna. Before a beginning student tries to take an external object for kasina, such as earth kasina, he or she should first enter the first, second, third, and fourth jhâna, preferably using the ânàpàna nimitta or white kasina as the object. Emerging from the fourth jhâna, the mind is very concentrated and powerful, thus making the task of taking a kasina as object, such as earth kasina, much easier. Once a yogi is proficient with a kasina, she or he needs only to pay attention to a previous image for the nimitta to arise.

The student initially locates the proper color for the kasina undertaken. The color or other characteristic (such as earth, water, fire, etc.) of the specific kasina is used as the meditative object when it can be seen by the student when his or her eyes are closed. When the jhâna factors are strengthening, the kasina becomes energized and clearly visible. The student can sense when the kasina becomes stable. The kasina is available whenever the student closes his or her eyes, even if for a moment. Once the image of the kasina is stable and energized, the student begins to expand the kasina. The kasina may expand on its own. If not, the student uses subtle meditative intention to expand the kasina.

The kasina is expanded a few inches at a time. Should the kasina become thin or the student see apparent holes in the kasina with the wisdom eye, the kasina has been expanded too quickly. The student uses meditative intention to retract the kasina to a smaller size that feels more stable. He or she meditates upon the kasina as an object until it is stable and the jhâna is energized. The jhâna factors specific to that kasina jhâna increase as before. As the jhâna factors for the specific jhâna become stronger, the kasina can eventually be expanded to encompass the entire world, including the student. Up to this point, while focusing on the kasina, the concentration is at the level of access concentration,

When the endless kasina color is independently stable and bright, the student is directed to focus on a small spot on the expanded kasina. This spot becomes the new object of meditation. This is like looking into the open, expansive sky and being transfixed upon a specific, particular spot. When meditative concentration is strong and all the jhâna factors needed for that jhâna are strong, the spot on the kasina draws the meditator into first jhâna. When all five jhâna masteries are attained for the first jhâna using a particular kasina as an object, the student is directed to the next successively higher jhâna until all four jhânas and the five masteries in each are completed using that kasina as an object.

We will refer back to this process with each kasina rather than laboriously restating it for each jhâna of each kasina. Again, the sequence initially cultivating the kasinas is as follows:

- White Kasina
- Nila Kasina
- Yellow Kasina
- Red Kasina
- Earth Kasina
- Water Kasina
- Fire Kasina
- Wind Kasina
- Light Kasina
- Space Kasina

WHITE KASINA

To start white kasina practice, the student once again goes through the first, second, third, and fourth jhânas using the ânàpàna nimitta as the object. Then the Thirty-Two Body Parts Meditation is quickly undertaken and completed. The skeleton is seen separate from the other parts of the Thirty-Two Body Parts Meditation and is taken up as a specific meditative object. The meditator uses the wisdom eye to locate the whitest part of the skeleton; often the back of the skull is taken as a meditative object given its color, size, and round shape (resembling a disc shape). The back of the skull's whiteness is then taken as the meditative object.

The white color taken from the back of the student's skull is seen where the nimitta previously appeared, when the student's eyes are closed in meditation. If the student cannot find the proper white to be taken as an object in his or her body, he or she uses the white from an object in nature—a cloud or other source, such as a flower. It needs to be a white that intuitively feels like the right color. From the strength of the fourth jhâna, the factors for first jhâna (vitakka, vicâra, piti, sukha, and ekaggatâ) begin to arise. At this time the white held as object begins to take a disc form. A white disc is then the natural object of meditation. This white object becomes a stable meditative object. The stability of the kasina is apparent by the independently energized, bright white kasina. The kasina is expanded to encompass the entire world. This may happen without any effort by the student. If the kasina does not automatically expand, the student slowly expands it in each meditation period by intention.

From the student's awareness, there is white in every direction, as far as the wisdom eye can see. The vast whiteness includes the student. When the expanded white is everywhere and that object is stable, the meditator takes a specific point in the white to place the meditative attention. Over time, your meditative attention effortlessly locks onto a specific, small spot on the expanded kasina. While this sounds strange to the thinking mind, when you are doing this, it is quite comfortable to do. The meditative attention falls naturally on a specific spot on the expanded white kasina and that becomes the new meditative object.

Eventually, as the jhâna factors increase, this spot on the expanded white kasina draws the student into jhâna. Alternatively, one can make a resolve for the jhâna. In the same process as before, the meditator progresses through the first, second, third, and fourth jhânas using white kasina as an object, discerning the jhâna factors after each meditation period in jhâna and staying with the particular jhâna until the five masteries for each jhâna have been achieved.

Again, if the student tries to move to the next jhâna or kasina without fully gaining all of the five jhâna masteries in each of the four jhânas using that particular kasina, it is impossible to take the next kasina in the sequence as an object and have it be stable enough for jhâna.

Patient, persistent practice with each jhâna is needed to continue working through the kasinas. After white kasina is used to enter the four jhânas, the white kasina now becomes the beginning meditative object for the remaining kasinas. This means that at the start of each meditation period, the student intentionally sees the white kasina. The white kasina is expanded, once stable and energized, until the jhâna factors for first jhâna are strong. The student then allows awareness to be drawn to a spot on the expanded white color. The spot taken on the fully expanded white color draws the student into first jhâna. The meditator passes through each of the first four jhânas using white kasina as an object prior to starting a new kasina.

Nila (Brown/Black/Blue) Kasina

The "nila" kasina is a color likened to brown, blue, black, or a combination of the three. The student finds there is an affinity with one of these colors or the blended color of "nila." Nila is based on the blue black of black head hair or the color of bile from the Thirty-Two Body Parts Meditation. If either of these is not the right color for a student, then a flower or other color in nature can be used. We found that a color closest to those found on or in the human body is best. For some reason, it is easier to hold as a meditative object.

Once again, each jhâna is undertaken using nila kasina as an object until the student attains the five masteries for each jhâna, including sitting three hours in one meditation period in each of the first four jhânas. The appropriate jhâna factors are discerned with the wisdom eye in the bhavanga after each meditation period in each successive jhâna. When the five jhâna masteries are achieved, the next jhâna is approached, cultivated, and entered as discussed previously in the general kasina section. When the student has successfully attained jhâna mastery in the fourth jhâna using nila kasina as an object, the student is ready for yellow kasina.

Yellow Kasina

Ven. Pa Auk Sayadaw usually directs the student to use his or her urine as the yellow color for yellow kasina. If this works, great. If not, then find a yellow flower or other object in nature that has the color you feel intuitively to be the proper yellow kasina color for this meditation. The student can confirm the correct color yellow has been located when it can be easily seen for an extended period of time with the eyes shut.

The student proceeds through each of the four jhânas using white kasina as an object, with its corresponding jhâna factors. After completing all four jhânas using white kasina, the student develops nila kasina. Next the student passes through each jhâna with its appropriate jhâna factors, using nila kasina as an object. The bhavanga is checked with the wisdom eye after each jhâna to ensure the proper jhâna factors were present.

Next, the meditator focuses on the yellow kasina until the first jhâna factors (vitakka, vicâra, piti sukha, and ekaggatâ) arise. When concentration is strong enough, the awareness is drawn into first jhâna using yellow kasina as an object. The student proceeds with each of the four jhânas as with the prior kasinas, gaining the five masteries with each jhâna. Once the five jhâna masteries are attained with the fourth jhâna using yellow kasina as an object, the student moves to red kasina.

Red Kasina

The student next seeks a red color that intuitively feels to be

JHÂNAS ADVICE FROM TWO SPIRITUAL FRIENDS

the right red color for a meditative object. Ven. Pa Auk Sayadaw recommends using the color of the student's blood, as seen in the Thirty-Two Body Parts Meditation. If the color of the student's blood does not easily become the color red for the kasina meditation, the student can find the proper color in nature—possibly a flower. There is no logical way to know the right red color. When the student sees the correct red for this meditation, she or he knows it.

The red color is taken as before as the meditative object. It is to be seen when the eyes are closed in the same way as the colors white, nila, and yellow for those kasinas. If the red color fades before becoming independently stable, the student opens her or his eyes to observe the red being used for the kasina color. When the red color can be seen with the eyes shut, the student resumes the meditation period. Once the red color has become the kasina, the student proceeds as before with expanding the red kasina. The student follows the same pattern with this kasina to each jhâna as before. When the five jhâna masteries for all four jhânas have been attained using red kasina as an object, the student is directed to develop earth kasina.

EARTH KASINA

We are now moving from color kasinas to kasinas based on the elements. We speculate that where the color kasina meditations based on body parts purify various energies and perceptions of the body, the elements kasina meditations purify perception of the elements that make up our environment—materiality.

In preparing for earth kasina, the student needs to find dirt that has a color representing the essence of earth to the student. A small amount of this dirt can be collected in a container. Alternatively, one can draw a circle on the ground outside and gaze at it for some minutes to imprint the visual image of the earth. Initially, the meditator observes the dirt with open eyes. Eventually, the image of earth needs to be independently held as a meditative object when the student's eyes are closed. The image, as well as the essence of earth, is then the meditative object for earth kasina. Essence can be described as the mind's feel of earth as the object. As one progresses through the remaining kasinas, both the image (when possible) and the essence of a kasina are the meditative objects of the particular kasina. This prepares the student to hold increasingly subtle kasinas as objects, as well as even more subtle meditative objects found in the formless jhânas.

When the earth image can be seen and held as a meditative object, the earth kasina meditation begins. With time, the jhâna factors arise for the first jhâna and the earth kasina becomes stable and energized independently. The kasina is then expanded as before, with the prior kasinas, and the process for entering and achieving the five jhâna masteries for each jhâna is implemented as it was in the prior kasina practice.

The meditator then proceeds through each of the first four jhânas following the same progression as with the prior kasinas. Each of the first through fourth jhânas is completed to the point of the five jhâna masteries, using earth kasina as an object. The student is then ready for water kasina.

WATER KASINA

Observing a bowl of water develops water kasina as a meditative object. It is helpful to use both the image of water as well as the subtle essence as the meditative object. For water, it is helpful to regard the essence as what remains when the color, movement, and properties of water are removed. When the water can be discerned with eyes closed, it is taken as the object of meditation. If while meditating the object slips away, the student resumes staring at the bowl of water with open eyes to recapture its image and essence as a meditative object.

When the student begins to perceive water with the eyes closed, water becomes the focus of meditation until it becomes a kasina. The five jhâna factors arise for first jhâna. The student then proceeds to expand the water kasina to cover the entire world, including the student. The student's meditative attention falls upon a small point on the expanded water kasina and through this spot enters first jhâna, following the same progression as with the prior kasinas.

The kasina progression is followed as outlined above. When the student has attained the five jhâna masteries in each of the first, second, third, and fourth jhânas using water kasina as an object, he or she is ready for fire kasina.

FIRE KASINA

To obtain fire as an object of meditation, the meditator can use a candle or other small flame. The flame is observed open-eyed for its image as well as its essence. Even though fire moves, it is possible to see it as a stable image with eyes closed. If the object cannot be seen with eyes closed, the meditator returns to observing the fire open-eyed. Once the object is seen clearly as a kasina with the eyes closed and the five jhâna factors have arisen, the fire kasina appears stable and energized. The fire kasina is expanded as before with the prior kasinas. The fire kasina is fully expanded to include the entire world as well as the student. As before, the meditative attention naturally falls upon a small point on the expanded fire kasina. This spot on the expanded fire kasina is taken as the meditative object drawing the student into first jhâna. When the five jhâna masteries are attained in the first jhâna using fire kasina as an object, the meditator proceeds with the kasina jhâna progression outlined above. Once the meditator has attained the five jhâna masteries for second, third, and fourth jhânas using fire kasina as an object, she or he proceeds with developing wind kasina.

WIND KASINA

Taking wind as an object is difficult to conceptually understand. This is why cultivating the essence of the prior elements kasinas can be helpful. The meditator should find a place where wind is blowing. Wind can be observed in a window, doorway, or outside blowing in bushes or trees. One can also feel the wind on one's skin. If one can see an image of wind in the mind's eye, that can be taken as an object. Alternately or in addition, one can take the essence of wind as the meditative object. To cultivate the essence, while watching or feeling the wind, we eliminate the sight and sensation of wind. What remains is close to the wind's essence.

The student takes wind as the object of meditation. Wind becomes a kasina. As the jhâna factors arise, the kasina becomes stable and energized. This energized kasina is expanded until it fills the entire world, including the student. When this expanded wind kasina is stable, the meditative attention is drawn to a small point on the expanded kasina. When the jhâna factors are of sufficient strength, the student is drawn into first jhâna. The five jhâna masteries for first jhâna need to be obtained before moving on to second jhâna using wind kasina as an object. The steps for the subsequent jhânas are outlined above.

Once the five jhâna masteries of the first, second, third, and fourth jhâna have been attained using wind kasina as an object, the meditator proceeds to light kasina.

LIGHT KASINA

The object for this kasina is light, which for some is seen as an image and for others moves closer to the essence of light. To obtain light as a meditative object, the student observes light streaming through a window or doorway. The attention is on the beam of light but not the particles that the light catches in the air. When clear morning sun is available, the sun disc may be used as light kasina object. Other times the sunlight that shines between tree branches or leaves may be suitable to use as a light kasina object. When closing one's eyes, one observes what remains as light. When light can be detected with eyes closed, the student then takes light as the meditative object. As the jhâna factors arise, light becomes a kasina. With further meditation, the light kasina becomes stable and independently energized. If the stable light kasina does not expand on its own, the student then expands it to cover the entire world, including the student. When this expanded light kasina is stable, the meditative attention falls upon a small point on the expanded light kasina. When all the jhâna factors are sufficiently strong and the time is ripe, the student is drawn into first jhâna. The meditator then follows the progression outlined to obtain the five jhâna masteries for the second, third, and fourth jhânas using light kasina as an object. This includes checking the bhavanga with the wisdom eye for the corresponding jhâna factors after exiting each jhâna.

When the five jhâna masteries have been obtained for the first, second, third, and fourth jhânas using light kasina as an object, the student proceeds to space kasina.

SPACE KASINA

With this kasina, the student takes space as the meditative object. The student can gaze at the night sky to attune to what is meant by "space." When the area between the stars is observed, the essence of space remains. Another option is to hold a round circle against a clear sky. The yogi pays attention to the space within the circle. Space is then held as a meditative object with the student's eyes closed. As the jhâna factors arise, space becomes a kasina. The student continues with meditation on the space kasina. When the jhâna factors and meditative concentration are sufficiently strong, the kasina becomes stable and independently energized. The space kasina is then expanded to cover the entire world, including the student. After the expanded space kasina is stabilized, the meditative attention shifts to a small point on the expanded space kasina. In time, the student enters first jhâna. Once the five jhâna masteries are obtained in the first jhâna using space kasina as an object, the student follows the progression outlined in the kasina section to gain the five jhâna masteries for the second, third, and fourth jhânas using space kasina as an object.

While still in the form realm, the space kasina is approaching the formless/immaterial jhânas. There is a qualitative difference in the progression of kasinas as each new kasina is more refined, subtle, and delicate as a meditative object. One can see this, as earth is much more dense than space. The student's localized consciousness is being refined and purified with each lighter and subtler kasina. This is preparing the student to approach the immaterial realms of the upper jhânas.

THE "BASE" MEDITATION OBJECT
AND "RECHARGING" CONCENTRATION

During practice of the kasinas, for some people, the "base" meditative object sometimes shifts from the ânàpànà nimitta to the white kasina. Ven. Pa Auk Sayadaw instructs that one can make this shift and use white kasina as the object while moving around in the world or can continue to use the ânàpànà nimitta as the base meditative object when one is eating, walking, and so on.

It can be helpful to use white kasina as a base because the earth kasina will be used repeatedly in the upper formless jhânas to access the Base of Boundless Space (the fifth jhâna). While it is possible to go straight to earth kasina, for most people white kasina is an easier starting point, given its similarity to the ânàpànà nimitta and its ability to be seen even while moving around, walking, eating, etc. Earth kasina is difficult to take as a base for many reasons, including its darker color. As such, this is not recommended. The ânàpànà nimitta is another alternative; however, it begins to feel somewhat gross compared to the white kasina at this point in the practice, which for some meditators makes white kasina more useful.

Stephen found that he preferred to use the ânàpànà nimitta as a meditative base while walking, eating, etc. When he sat for formal meditation, white kasina arose naturally and provided easy access to earth kasina. Tina found that the white kasina arose naturally as an ongoing base at this point. However, over the many days of progressing through all the lower jhânas and kasinas, it was beneficial for her to return to the ânàpànà nimitta periodically to "charge up" the concentration.

Especially before moving on from one kasina to another, it is important to have a strong, laser-like concentration. Therefore, returning to a meditation period with the ânàpànà nimitta as the object can be worthwhile and even prevent the progression from wobbling. Because the ânàpànà nimitta has the ever-present physical sensation of the breath, it is always easily accessible. Alternately, when one is undertaking a sitting period and progressing through several jhânas as one moves to the higher kasinas, spending a few extra minutes in the first jhâna with ânàpànà nimitta can also create the jhâna "rocket fuel" necessary to maintain a solid progression.

We have now reviewed all the meditative practices through the fourth form jhâna. The student has now attained the five jhâna masteries of the four form jhânas. It is now time to continue our journey into the four formless jhânas—the immaterial states that provide gateways to direct perception of emptiness (sunnata), unity (consciousness), and that which is beyond emptiness and unity.

CHAPTER 4

IMMATERIAL STATES/ FORMLESS JHÂNAS (FIVE THROUGH EIGHT) AND RELATED PRACTICES

For awareness to be absorbed into a formless or "immaterial" jhâna is among the most delicate of Buddhist practices and subtle meditations. The realms traversed are breathtaking in their vastnesses and sheer depth of being. These are the source of "all is one," "all is nothing," and "all is both nothing and one, and neither nothing or one—at once." This is the terrain presented here. The objects of meditation in these formless realms are too insubstantial for imagination. Fortunately, they can be experienced directly. The four formless jhânas are:

- The Base of Boundless Space (the fifth jhâna)
- The Base of Boundless Consciousness (the sixth jhâna)
- The Base of Nothingness (the seventh jhâna)
- The Base of Neither Perception Nor Non-perception (the eighth jhâna)

In some texts, these meditations are not referred to as "jhânas" because they are thought not to be true absorptions. Rather, it is thought that they are actual, objective, nonmaterial (formless) realms that are accessed by awareness through the gateways of the meditative object. The laser-like concentration developed in the lower jhânas and kasinas becomes the "key" to opening these gateways to the formless realms. Our experience was that they do indeed experientially feel more like "immaterial realms" than like meditative absorptions. However, because there is a progression of practice and for ease of language, we will refer to them primarily as formless jhânas and only occasionally as immaterial states or realms.

Only after the student has attained the five jhâna masteries for each of the first four form jhânas using each of the ten kasinas as an object does the teacher direct the student to the formless jhânas. By this time the student has discovered and utilized each of the ten kasinas as a meditative object for each form jhâna. Each successive kasina, as the object for accessing the form jhânas, is lighter in appearance and more delicately subtle in its essence. Furthermore, the student has spent a minimum of three uninterrupted hours in each of the four form jhânas for each of the ten kasinas. Usually there have been several attempts before time mastery is achieved.

This is an enormous amount of time to spend fully absorbed in the jhânas and in access concentration leading to absorption. The student's meditative concentration has become stronger and increasingly focused and laser-like. Also, moving from kasina to kasina and developing the specific jhâna factors for each of the four form jhânas with each kasina demands the development of tremendous meditative skill, flexibility of mind, and promotes a nearly continuous personal purification. Building progressive concentration on this number of objects and attaining the five masteries in each provides a solid foundation from which to attempt access to the immaterial realms.

To start, most meditators will use white kasina as the beginning object and then move to earth kasina, which provides access to the Base of Boundless Space. The jhâna factors for the fourth form jhâna (ekaggatâ and upekkhâ) are the same remaining jhâna factors for each of the formless jhânas. Once the meditator has progressed through each of the form jhânas using this method and attained the five jhâna masteries in each formless jhâna, he or she will use all of the other kasinas to also progress through the formless jhânas, with the exception of space kasina. Space kasina cannot be used because of its relationship to the Base of Boundless Space (the fifth jhâna). One cannot use space as a kasina to enter space as an immaterial state. The five jhâna masteries are also attained for each kasina in each upper jhâna, as it was in the four form jhânas.

The kasinas used to experience the formless jhânas are in a different order than for the lower four form jhânas. The order of the kasinas is changed for the formless jhânas to continuously refine and purify the student's consciousness. The order of the kasinas in the formless jhânas is:

- Earth Kasina
- Water Kasina
- Fire Kasina
- Wind Kasina
- Nila Kasina
- Yellow Kasina
- Red Kasina
- White kasina
- Light Kasina

BASE OF BOUNDLESS SPACE (THE FIFTH JHÂNA)

Proceeding from the base meditative object of either the
ânàpànà nimitta or the white kasina, the meditator now takes
earth kasina as a meditative object. If earth kasina is difficult to see
as an object for first jhâna, the meditator returns to white kasina
practice. White kasina is taken as a meditative object and the jhâna
factors for first jhâna (vitakka, vicâra, piti, sukha, and ekaggatâ)
are cultivated. The meditator proceeds through the first, second,
third, and fourth jhânas using white kasina as an object, remaining
in each until stability is attained and the five jhâna masteries are
reached. At this point, stability in the lower four jhânas are likely
to be established in thirty minutes or less.

When earth kasina can be taken as a meditative object and the
jhâna factors are cultivated, the meditator enters first jhâna. When
stability is reached in first jhâna using earth kasina as an object, the
meditator moves to second jhâna (with the jhâna factors of piti,
sukha, and ekaggatâ) with earth kasina as the meditative object.
When second jhâna stabilizes, the meditator continues to third
jhâna (with sukha and ekaggatâ as the jhâna factors). When third
jhâna has stabilized, the meditator moves to fourth jhâna (with
the jhâna factors of ekaggatâ and upekkhâ). The meditator enters
and experiences stability in this fourth jhâna using earth kasina as
an object.

While in access concentration near fourth jhâna, using earth
kasina as an object, the meditator next directs awareness to
the *space* the expanded earth kasina *occupies*. This is sometimes
accomplished by seeing either small, minute holes in the earth
kasina or an edge of the earth kasina—a seam where space and the
earth kasina meet. Stephen found applying attention to the edge
of the earth kasina easier. Tina found the holes method easier. By
focusing on either the small holes in the kasina or the edge of the

kasina, the student directs his or her meditative attention to the *space* the earth kasina occupies, by seeing either the holes or the seam where the kasina and space meet. By focusing on the space the kasina occupies and removing attention from the earth kasina, the earth kasina is "removed."

How the earth kasina leaves the space is not something to which the student pays any attention. The student should have confidence that when space is effectively taken as a meditative object, the earth kasina is not present. The important aspect at this point of the meditation is that earth kasina is removed, leaving the space it formerly occupied. The meditator then directs the subtle awareness of the space to expand to encompass the entire world, or infinite universe, including the student, if the space is not already expanded from holding the expanded earth kasina.

When the jhâna factors of ekaggatâ and upekkhâ are strong and the bright, jhâna energy is sufficiently concentrated and the meditator's attention focuses on a small spot in the unending expanded space. There is a spot that for some reason draws the attention quite naturally and easily. This small spot in the field of space then becomes the meditative object.

With sufficient time meditating on the "attention spot" in the field of unending space, the meditator is drawn into full absorption into the Base of Boundless Space (the fifth jhâna). The Base of Boundless Space is the source of unending, unbounded, unlimited space in a formless realm. Being absorbed into the Base of Boundless Space is quite exquisite and qualitatively far more refined than the fourth jhâna of space kasina. This is the space in which all objects in the form realm appear. Perhaps we can conceptually liken it to the canvas of life in which each brushstroke of life appears. It is a very profound experience.

As with the other jhânas, the meditator achieves the five jhâna masteries of this jhâna before moving to the Base of Boundless Consciousness (the sixth jhâna) as a meditative object. Jhâna mastery includes one meditation period of three continuous hours in the Base of Boundless Space uninterrupted. This is likely to take several attempts before the time mastery is achieved. The formless jhânas are a purer energy than the form jhânas. The purification and refinement of the personal consciousness can be a very intense experience. Until the refinement of personal consciousness is complete in the Base of Boundless Space, the student is not able to access the Base of Boundless Consciousness. When the five jhâna masteries have been attained in the Base of Boundless Space, the student can proceed to access the Base of Boundless Consciousness.

BASE OF BOUNDLESS CONSCIOUSNESS (THE SIXTH JHÂNA)

Proceeding from the base object of either the ânàpànà nimitta or the white kasina, the meditator takes earth kasina as a meditative object and enters the first, second, third, and fourth jhânas using earth kasina as an object. Earth kasina is expanded as before to encompass the entire world. At this point, the jhâna factors of ekaggatâ and upekkhâ are present, as is true in the fourth jhâna and all of the formless jhânas.

As before, the meditative attention moves to the space the earth kasina occupies, either by seeing tiny holes in the earth kasina or by focusing on the edge of the earth kasina where it meets space. The earth kasina is removed, and the new object of the Base of Boundless Space arises.

Once again taking Boundless Space as a meditative object, the student meditates upon expanding the awareness of unending space, if it is not already fully expanded. The meditator next allows his or her meditative attention to be drawn to a particular small spot in Boundless Space. When meditative concentration, upekkhâ and ekaggatâ are of sufficient strength, the meditator becomes fully absorbed into the Base of Boundless Space (the fifth jhâna).

The meditator then directs his or her attention to the *consciousness* that *holds* boundless space as its object. An object such as the consciousness of boundless space is very difficult to speak about or imagine as a concept. Once the meditator has completed the absorption into Base of Boundless Space (the fifth jhâna), taking the *consciousness* of boundless space as a meditative object is subtle, yet apparent and somehow possible.

Naturally, the universal mind/awareness that holds unending space as its object is a very subtle object itself, while also being very refined. When the meditator is at this point in the jhâna practice, the consciousness of the Base of Boundless Space can indeed be taken as an object.

The consciousness that holds the Base of Boundless Space is taken as an object. The consciousness holding the object is impossible to extend because it is by its nature infinite. As before in the fifth jhâna, this consciousness holding boundless space is stabilized during meditation. The jhâna factors of ekaggatâ and upekkhâ are held until of the necessary strength. Once the consciousness holding boundless, unending space is known as the meditative object and ekaggatâ and upekkhâ are strong, the attention can hold the entirety of this consciousness. Concentration and one-pointedness deepen and stabilize on this extremely subtle meditative object.

When ripe, the meditator is drawn into full absorption in the Base of Boundless Consciousness (the sixth jhâna). This boundless, unending consciousness contains everything. This is the consciousness of unified oneness. Everything is contained within the one consciousness here and this one consciousness pervades everywhere endlessly. It is an undivided wholeness. It is unity. The purification of awareness facilitated by full absorption into the Base of Boundless Consciousness that holds all of unity is profound.

As with the prior jhânas, the five jhâna masteries must be attained in the Base of Boundless Consciousness before it is completed. Once all five masteries are reached in the sixth jhâna, including a single three-hour uninterrupted absorption in the Base of Boundless Consciousness, the student is directed towards the Base of Nothingness.

BASE OF NOTHINGNESS (THE SEVENTH JHÂNA)

The object for the Base of Nothingness is the *absence* of the *consciousness* of Boundless Space. So, in effect, the new object is the absence of the object used for the sixth jhâna. The student goes through the first four jhânas using earth kasina. If earth kasina is difficult to take as a meditative object, the meditator begins with white kasina and follows the proper steps to establish each of the first four jhânas using white kasina as an object. The meditator remains in each of the first four jhânas using white kasina as an object until stability is known there.

If the meditator can easily see earth kasina with eyes closed, then he or she proceeds accordingly through the first four jhânas using earth kasina as an object. The time spent in the four lower jhânas in earth kasina is only long enough to establish stability, perhaps five to ten minutes each. The student then reestablishes the Base of Boundless Space by removing the earth kasina. Then, again, the consciousness of the fifth jhâna, Base of Boundless Space, is taken as an object and full absorption into the sixth jhâna arises.

The student stays in the jhâna long enough to reach stability. The stability in the upper formless jhânas takes longer than the lower four jhânas as the upper jhânas are much more refined.

When stability is reached in the Base of Boundless Consciousness, the student takes up the Base of Nothingness by focusing on the *absence* of the *consciousness* of Boundless Space. Two mind moments do not arise simultaneously. When the consciousness of the Base of Boundless Space is present, the Base of Boundless Consciousness is absent. Again, when the base of Boundless Consciousness is present, then the consciousness of the Base of Boundless Space is absent. That absence of consciousness of the base of Boundless Space is used as the object for the seventh jhâna.

The nothingness of this immaterial state, the seventh jhâna, is complete, unending emptiness. Emptiness is a rich fullness of *no identity* and *no thing*. It is "no-thing-ness." Usually with forms (such as thoughts, people, and objects) there are many ways that we mark the form with identity. We can have a certain feeling or relationship to it. In the Base of Nothingness, *all* sense of any form or structure, as well as *any* markers of identity, are gone. This is a dramatic shift. The Base of Boundless Consciousness is bursting full of the consciousness of everything—all is welcome in the oneness. In contrast, the Base of Nothingness is the utter void, the "dazzling darkness."

This is not an unpleasant jhâna. There is a sense of pristine purity, of freedom here. Despite being no-thing-ness, there is a sense of presence—a deep, still, pervasive peace. It is the experience of no-thing from which everything (consciousness) can arise and be supported.

When the absence of the consciousness of the fifth jhâna of boundless space can be held, it becomes the meditative object. This may require many attempts, as the object is so fine it can easily slip away. Holding this object is like holding gauze up to the sky. It is an object that is delicately held. When ready, the object becomes stable and attention focuses on a particular spot within this nothingness. Certainly, having any specific location in vast, primordial nothingness sounds preposterous. Yet when at this stage, it is exactly what occurs.

Once awareness is deeply concentrated on this one location, in the already expanded *absence* of the *consciousness* of boundless space, and the jhâna factors of ekaggatâ and upekkhâ are strongly present, the meditator is drawn into full absorption in this immaterial state. As with the prior jhânas, the student continues with this jhâna until the five jhâna masteries have been achieved, including a single three-hour uninterrupted absorption in this jhâna.

With each of the formless jhânas, a tremendous amount of purification occurs. The student's mind stream is directly entering and being suffused by the source of consciousness and the source of the emptiness from which consciousness arises. To be fully absorbed in these realms, beyond access concentration, is indescribable. These are sublime realms unimaginable to the thinking mind. Until these are personally and deeply experientially known, the student must take the existence of these immaterial states on faith in the Buddha and the jhâna teachers.

After the meditator has attained the five jhâna masteries in the Base of Nothingness, the student is ready for the next formless jhâna: the Base of Neither Perception Nor Non-perception.

BASE OF NEITHER PERCEPTION
NOR NON-PERCEPTION (THE EIGHTH JHÂNA)

The meditator takes earth kasina as the meditative object. If earth kasina is difficult to begin with as a meditative object, the meditator can start with white kasina. White kasina is then developed as before through the first four jhânas using white kasina as an object, until stability is reached in each.

When earth kasina can be taken as a meditative object, first jhâna is developed and entered. When stability in first jhâna is reached, the meditator develops and enters second jhâna using earth kasina as an object. As stability is obtained in second jhâna, third jhâna is developed and stabilized, and then fourth jhâna. After stability in fourth jhâna is reached using earth kasina as an object, the meditator goes through the process of removing earth kasina as the object. Again, the meditator's focus of attention is either minute holes in the earth kasina or the edge of earth kasina.

As before, earth kasina is removed and the space earth kasina formerly occupied is taken as a meditative object. When the jhâna factors of ekaggatâ and upekkhâ are strong, the meditator's attention shifts to a small spot in boundless space and focuses on this as the object. At the appropriate time, the meditator is drawn into the Base of Boundless Space.

The consciousness holding the Base of Boundless Space will become stable as a meditative object and the jhâna factors of ekaggatâ and upekkhâ will become strong. When ripe, the meditator's awareness is drawn into full absorption in the sixth jhâna, the Base of Boundless Consciousness. Upon exiting the sixth jhâna, the meditator takes the *absence* of the Base of Consciousness as the meditative object.

The absence of the Consciousness of the Base of Boundless Space will eventually be held as a meditative object, and the jhâna factors of ekaggatâ and upekkhâ will become strong. When the meditator's concentration is ripe, the Base of Nothingness draws the meditator's consciousness into full absorption in the seventh jhâna. Upon exiting the seventh jhâna, the meditator proceeds toward the eighth jhâna—the base of Neither Perception Nor Non-perception.

The meditator now takes the *consciousness* of the Base of

Nothingness as the meditative object. The meditator shifts
attention away from the Base of Nothingness and focuses on
the consciousness *holding* nothingness. This "consciousness of
nothing" is the container in which nothingness is held. This is an
even finer gauze-like object. To hold an object as subtle and fine
as this, the meditator's sense of "me" must be almost completely
transparent. Taking the consciousness of the Base of Nothingness
as a meditative object is like holding a spider's web to the sky. It
is a very delicate, exquisitely fragile object of awareness. Only a
purified, jhâna-energized awareness can hold the object of the
Base of Neither Perception Nor Non-perception.

The *consciousness* of the Base of Nothingness is taken as a
meditative object. With time, the jhâna factors of ekaggatâ,
upekkhâ, and the meditator's concentration become strong. With
prolonged meditation, the meditator's awareness is eventually
drawn into full absorption in the Base of Neither Perception Nor
Non-perception, the eighth jhâna.

This jhâna cannot begin to be imagined or conceptualized.
While being outside perception and non-perception, this realm
contains both and neither—at the same time! It is a direct
experience of non-dual awareness. There is neither perception
nor non-perception in this immaterial state. This immaterial state
is beyond a sense of mentality; the mind absolutely cannot grasp
it. The usual sense of thinking cannot be present here, not even
in access concentration. If it arises, the Base of Neither Perception
Nor Non-perception wafts away, like a wisp of smoke.

The first time each of us experienced this realm it was
unimaginably spectacular. For Tina, it was so intense that she could
only tolerate a few minutes the first few times before awareness
settled and there was a complete surrender to its purification and
subtlety. Stephen was knocked out of the jhâna after about one and

a half hours. His awareness could not have remained in the Base of Neither Perception Nor Non-perception one second longer at that time. This was less than was needed for jhâna mastery. Yet, even the first experience of this jhâna was akin to being completely reborn as a new, innocent, pure being.

Once the five jhâna masteries are attained, including one uninterrupted meditation period of three hours, the student has completed the eighth jhâna, the Base of Neither Perception Nor Non-perception, and can proceed to the other kasinas.

ORDER OF KASINAS THROUGH THE IMMATERIAL JHÂNAS

The kasinas in the formless jhânas are completed in the following order:

- Earth Kasina
- Water Kasina
- Fire Kasina
- Wind Kasina
- Nila Kasina
- Yellow Kasina
- Red Kasina
- White Kasina
- Light Kasina

The meditator takes up the remaining eight kasinas (space kasina is excluded) as the object of entry to the four formless jhânas. The meditator progresses using each kasina as the object through the four formless jhânas, progressing through the four formless jhânas of the Base of Boundless Space, the Base of Boundless Consciousness, the Base of Nothingness, and the Base of Neither Perception Nor Non-perception. The student achieves the five jhâna masteries with *each* of the formless jhânas through *each* kasina, including one meditation period of three hours in each immaterial state/formless jhâna with each kasina.

The student begins by taking the kasina as an object into first jhâna. This is done as quickly as the jhâna can be stabilized using that kasina as an object. The student then takes the specific kasina through the second, third, and fourth jhânas, also one at a time. As before, upon exiting jhâna the student checks the bhavanga with the wisdom eye to confirm the requisite jhâna factors are present. Over time, the student moves through each lower jhâna in a matter of a few minutes.

Once all lower jhânas are completed with the specific kasina, the instructions for accessing each upper jhâna is followed as described with earth kasina. Complete the first four jhânas using the particular kasina and then either see tiny holes or focus on the edge where the kasina touches space. Then, remove the kasina to reveal the space that holds it as the Base of Boundless Space. Proceed as previously described through the four upper jhânas.

The element (earth, water, fire, and air) kasinas are completed first to purify and loosen the student's connection to the elements in her or his body and all of materiality. Then the color kasinas are completed from darkest to lightest. This is done also to refine the student's consciousness for the light kasina, which is the most refined of the kasinas in the formless jhânas. Using the light kasina as an entry point leading to the delicacy of the eighth jhâna of Neither Perception Nor Non-perception is an exquisitely refined and subtle experience.

The purification that occurs in the formless upper jhânas is delicate, yet *very* concentrated and intense. The student must have a willingness to allow the purity to penetrate her or his entire being and life. We can attest that when the five jhâna masteries are attained, using the final light kasina and completing the final jhâna of the Base of Neither Perception Nor Non-perception, there is a deep and profound *knowing* of never being the same person again. The purification continues working on the student and later manifests in the student's life in unexpected ways that change the beliefs, opinions, habits, and behavior of the student. We feel even now, several years after attaining the five jhâna masteries for all eight jhânas, the purification continues to unfold and deepen.

More importantly, this practice has altered the ongoing experiential awareness of the manifestation of all that we see—from our own body-minds to the material world around us. There is an ongoing perception that all this manifests from the mystery of the unconditioned, down through the formless realms, into the form realms, and eventually appears as materiality—as the words on this page and your perception of them. Even when the daily experience of jhâna absorption is past, this visceral knowing remains, affecting each moment of experience and its relationship to the mystery.

We have now traversed the most delicate of meditations. With this very pristine, refined concentration and purification as a foundation, we will now move into the Protective Meditations, which prepare one to eventually undertake the Vipassana practice.

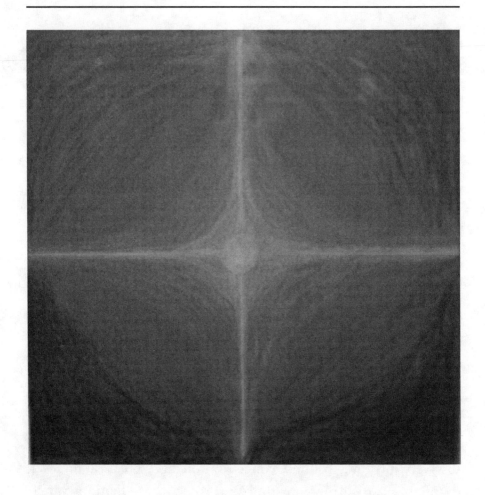

Essence of the Eighth Jhana, drawn by Tina Rasmussen

CHAPTER 5

THE SUBLIME ABIDINGS AND PROTECTIVE MEDITATIONS

Now that the meditator has completed the jhânas' progression through the eighth jhâna, the next stage of practice is to complete the Sublime Abidings and Protective Meditations.

The Four Sublime Abidings (Bramaviharas) consist of the following meditation subjects:

- Mettâ (lovingkindness)
- Karunâ (compassion)
- Mudita (joy)
- Upekkhâ (equanimity)

The Four Protective Meditations are the meditation subjects of:

- Mettâ (lovingkindness)
- Recollection of the Buddha
- Foulness Meditation
- Recollection of Death

The primary purpose of all of these practices is to provide a solid base of support for the practitioner as she or he progresses toward the insight practice of Vipassana. Because the insights that arise in Vipassana are deeply uprooting to the meditator's sense of self and of materiality and mentality as they have been previously known, the experience can be destabilizing. The protective meditations serve various purposes in providing and stabilizing the meditator's practice and encouraging the meditator to continue on in the face of this destabilization—which is essential for the realization of things as they truly are.

The Sublime Abidings provide a sense of well-being to clear one's karma with others and build the equanimity necessary for the letting go that happens in Vipassana. The Recollection of the Buddha provides inspiration and a direct feeling of connection to the Buddha as one who has completed this practice to its full fruition and whose teachings have guided thousands of practitioners through the ages. The Foulness Meditation (meditation on a corpse) softens one's attachment to oneself as the body. And the Recollection of Death stimulates an urgency of practice; it shows that there is no time to waste in realizing the truth because we never know when this life may end. Though these may sound like very traditional practices to Westerners, they are well worth doing and provide a variety of benefits to the meditator as a foundation for Vipassana and may even be returned to as necessary as one needs them during the Vipassana practice.

A secondary purpose of these practices is to continue deepening the faculty of concentration by providing additional meditation objects that can lead to various levels of concentration. With each of the above meditation subjects, Ven. Pa Auk Sayadaw asks his students to obtain the following level of concentration:

- Mettâ (lovingkindness)—third jhâna
- Karunâ (compassion)—third jhâna
- Mudîtâ (joy)—third jhâna
- Upekkhâ (equanimity)—fourth jhâna
- Recollection of the Buddha—access concentration
- Foulness Meditation—first jhâna
- Recollection of Death—access concentration

The first three Sublime Abidings are available only up to the third jhâna because they have an intrinsic sense of joy and happiness that is not present in the fourth jhâna. Upekkhâ (equanimity) can be used as a meditative subject up to the fourth jhâna because the remaining jhâna factors in the fourth jhâna are one-pointedness and equanimity. These four objects of the Sublime Abidings build on each other sequentially, so the culmination of this practice is the fourth jhâna in the practice of Upekkhâ (equanimity).

With the additional three protective meditations, only access concentration or first jhâna are possible. For this reason, the Sayadaw encourages the meditator to spend only one to two hours on this practice at a time so as not to dissipate the high concentration of the jhânas.

While completing these practices, the meditator also must continue jhâna meditation for one sitting per day completing up to the eighth jhâna. This ensures that intensive jhâna level concentration is available for use with these and other practices and does not dissipate over time.

Each of these practices is done by beginning with the ânàpàna nimitta or white kasina as the object, up to the fourth jhâna. Because the meditator has already completed a long period of time with the form and formless jhânas using the ânàpàna nimitta and the kasinas as primary objects, this is easy to do. Establishment of the fourth jhâna before beginning the Sublime Abidings and Protective Meditations ensures that the powerful concentration is present at the start and makes the establishment of the highest possible level of concentration on these new subjects easier.

Details of these meditation practices are outlined thoroughly in Ven. Pa Auk Sayadaw's book *Knowing and Seeing,* so will not be presented here. The Sublime Abidings (Bramaviharas) are taught widely in the West, and the Ven. Pa Auk Sayadaw's instruction on the practice is very similar with minor variations.

Once the practitioner has completed the Sublime Abidings and Protective Meditations, she or he is ready to proceed to the Four Elements Meditation and move toward the beginning of the Vipassana practice.

CHAPTER 6

FOUR ELEMENTS MEDITATION

Four Elements Meditation is a critical practice to develop well. All students of the Ven. Pa Auk Sayadaw must develop this meditation to undertake the Vipassana portion of the Buddha's Path. In this practice, we experientially learn and know that all that appears "real," including our own bodies, are comprised of a combination of the four elements. The belief in, and attachment to, the body becomes difficult to sustain after this practice is thoroughly experienced.

There are two ways in which a student undertakes the Four Elements Meditation. For those who have completed the practices as outlined in the book, the Four Elements Meditation is the next practice in the sequence. Those students who *can* attain jhâna using the Ânàpànàsati Meditation take up Four Elements Meditation *after* the Sublime Abidings and Protective Meditations discussed previously. The Sublime Abidings and Protective Meditations are undertaken to allow the student greater ease in facing the rigors of the kalàpa practice that come as a result of the Four Elements. The Four Elements Meditation then serves as the bridge that completes the Samatha practices and begins the Vipassana practice. These practitioners would be considered "Samatha yogis."

Ven. Pa Auk Sayadaw teaches that if someone finds, after exhaustive effort, that she or he cannot progress through the jhânas beginning with the Ânàpànàsati practice, the student may be directed to try Four Elements Meditation. (This is why our Practices Chart reflects the Four Elements as an alternate beginning point to Ânàpànàsati Meditation.) These practitioners would be considered "Vipassana yogis" or "Dry-insight yogis" as they are proceeding directly to the Vipassana practice.

The Four Elements Meditation allows the student to experience his or her body as being entirely composed of a compilation of the four elements. It is not possible to attain jhâna using the four elements as an object, as they are objects of momentary concentration. However, Four Elements Meditation *can* lead to access concentration.

Four Elements Meditation in its later application is used to directly discern (see) and analyze *rupa- kalàpas*. Rupa-kalàpas are tiny subatomic particles that make up all objects in the world of form. We will not discuss using Four Elements Meditation beyond the point of seeing kalàpas because we believe it is important to do that practice with a teacher who can guide the student in the intricacies of examining and analyzing materiality (rupa-kalàpas) and mentality (nama-kalàpas).

FOUR ELEMENTS MEDITATION

The four elements are: earth, water, fire, and air, with their associated characteristics.

- *Earth Element: hardness, roughness, heaviness, softness, smoothness, lightness*
- *Water Element: flowing, cohesion*
- *Fire Element: heat, coldness*
- *Wind Element: supporting, pushing*

We will present these in an order that we think is easier to learn. After learning the pairs in this way, the meditator should then complete the Four Elements Meditation in the traditional order. Pairing each element with its opposite allows an easier initial progression through the characteristics of each of the Four Elements. The progression is:

- *hardness, softness*
- *roughness, smoothness*
- *heaviness, lightness*
- *flowing, cohesion*
- *heat, coldness*
- *supporting, pushing*

To begin the Four Elements practice, the student should use white kasina as an object to progress through the first, second, third, and fourth jhânas. With the laser-like concentration of the fourth jhâna, the student seeks all *hardness* in his or her body. Examples of hardness are teeth, bones, and nails. The student must experientially locate each area of hardness in his or her body. When all areas of hardness in the body can be found and held simultaneously without division or distraction, the student then begins searching her or his body for *softness*, ignoring *hardness* entirely at this time.

Softness is everything that is *not hardness*. Literally, the experience in the body during this pairing is either of *hardness* or of *softness* when evaluating just these two characteristics of earth element. If you can easily hold *hardness*, you can shift your attention to everywhere else in your body to find all that is *softness*. The meditator then alternates between *hardness* and *softness* until each can be discerned and felt literally in an instant. *Hardness* and *softness* are next held distinctly and simultaneously.

Next the meditator examines the characteristics of *roughness* and *smoothness*. *Roughness* is discovered through the meditative awareness in the body. An example of *roughness* might be the tough skin on the bottom of your feet. All *roughness* in the body is discovered and experienced. This is done until all *roughness* in the body can be felt at once everywhere in the body.

Smoothness can be found by running the tongue over your lip, as one example. The tongue also feels quite smooth on the teeth. *Smoothness* is sought everywhere in the student's body. The student then alternates between *roughness* and *smoothness*. When the student can find *roughness* and *smoothness* quickly, both separately and simultaneously, the student advances to *heaviness* and *lightness*.

Heaviness can be felt where the bottom of your body (i.e., legs, feet, or buttocks) touches the meditation cushion, chair, or floor. Once this is known everywhere in the body at once, the student shifts his or her meditative awareness to *lightness*. One example of how *lightness* might be experienced is the hair on the student's arms. The student continues to explore the body, searching everywhere for *lightness*. When *lightness* and *heaviness* can be sensed clearly throughout the body, they are sensed quickly shifting from one to the other. *Heaviness* and *lightness* are then held simultaneously and distinctly.

Flowing and *cohesion* are the next characteristics the student looks for in the body. *Flowing* can be sensed as the blood or other liquids moving throughout your body, as an example. All areas of flowing need to be detected in the body. Each area of *flowing* needs to be felt at once before moving the attention to cohesion. *Cohesion* is felt as how the body holds itself together. The various muscles, blood vessels, and organs remarkably stay within the skin of this body. *Cohesion* must be felt everywhere in the body at once. The student then alternates between *flowing* and *cohesion*.

When each of these can be experienced completely in one instant, the student shifts to feeling both of these together distinctly and simultaneously.

Heat and *coldness* should not need any explanation. It is fairly easy to find these characteristics in your body. Again, these are experienced alternatingly until each can be distinctly experienced simultaneously with the other in an instant.

Supporting and *pushing* are a little tricky to find. *Supporting* is how the various organs are supported by their location, food or water consumed, and other factors you discover. Likewise, *pushing* can be felt when the breath is drawn into the body with deep deliberation. The wind pushes against the lungs and body allowing the body to breathe. The body is explored to find every area of *supporting*. Then once all areas of *supporting* are found, the student shifts the attention to *pushing*, locating all places of *pushing* in the body. As these are discerned and known deeply, the meditator alternates the attention from *supporting* to *pushing* and back again. Each characteristic should be felt as completely distinct from the other characteristic and then discerned simultaneously.

Once the student can easily identify each characteristic in each of the four elements, he or she proceeds to locating these characteristics in the traditionally prescribed order.

ORDER OF CHARACTERISTICS OF EACH ELEMENT PER TRADITIONAL INSTRUCTION

After all the characteristics are learned in the above order, the student begins to locate the characteristics of each element in the following order as is done traditionally. Again, the order of the traditional instruction is:

- *Earth Element: hardness, roughness, heaviness, softness, smoothness, lightness*

- *Water Element: flowing, cohesion*
- *Fire Element: heat, coldness*
- *Wind Element: supporting, pushing*

Once all characteristics are sufficiently experienced separately, they are experienced as an entire element. For example, the characteristics of the Water Element are *flowing* and *cohesion*. Once these are learned separately, the student needs to sense them simultaneously in the body holding them as *Water Element.*

When each characteristic is experienced for each element, the student cycles through each element, feeling all its characteristics separately at once. When each element, with all its characteristics, can be held, the student proceeds to run through the elements in order of *earth, water, fire,* and *air.* When each element can be distinctly felt in the body, the student cycles through all the elements to the point where he or she can do three complete rounds of all the elements in a minute, with each element being distinctly experienced. The meditator is likely to experience the body as a combination of these elements, not a distinct body. There is no part of the body that is not within one characteristic of an element. The time comes when the meditator can hold each element with its distinctness with all the other elements at once.

At this point, we were instructed by Ven. Pa Auk Sayadaw to use the wisdom eye to obtain a vantage point slightly above and behind the body, as if one is looking slightly down on one's body from just above and in back of the head. With continued deep meditation on the four elements, a light develops, a kind of glow around the body. The student does not shift the meditative attention to the glow but allows it to develop on its own. Our experience, at this point, was of seeing the entire body in its four elements, as a white, cloud-like form. Despite the white, cloud-like form, the student continues to maintain meditative attention on the four elements. Over time this white form begins to become crystal-like.

The white form transmutes into a perceived crystal body—the student's crystal body. Over time, the crystal body becomes brilliant in its glow and is perceived as diamond hard. This diamond-like body begins to glow a brilliant light. The light expands in every direction. The emanating light can be seen by the student during meditation. At this time the brilliant crystal body feels very clear and pure.

As with many of these practices, we were not sure what would happen when we started or what to expect. But, by staying true to the practice and maintaining awareness on the object, the practice did progress as described.

VARIATIONS ON HOW AND WHEN TO DO THIS PRACTICE

Stephen did this practice at the beginning, before going on to the Ânàpànàsati practice. As mentioned earlier, the teacher encourages students to do the Ânàpànàsati Meditation first, and if they are not successful, to try the Four Elements practice. In Stephen's case, because of physical issues, he did Four Elements Meditation first. This enabled energies in the body to smooth out before undertaking the Ânàpànàsati Meditation.

In Tina's case, she completed the practices in the sequence given by Ven. Pa Auk Sayadaw in his book *Knowing and Seeing*. As such, meditators who are doing the Four Elements after having completed all of the jhânas, kasinas, related practices, and protective meditations should also continue practicing the jhânas up to the eighth jhâna during one meditation period each day to maintain a high level of jhâna concentration. This makes for a very powerful, laser-like entry into the beginning of the Vipassana practice, starting with the Four Elements Meditation. It assures that the concentration developed over the many days, weeks, and months of practice is sustained and available to use in the Vipassana portion of the Buddhist path.

The Four Elements Meditation is very different from jhâna practice, in that it is fast moving and requires the use of momentary concentration rather than absorption. The meditator does not experience absorption in doing the Four Elements Meditation. He or she uses momentary concentration to develop a high level of access concentration. Practicing the jhânas (four form jhânas and four formless jhânas) at one sitting per day allows for a high level of concentration, then switching to doing the Four Elements Meditation practice for the rest of the day.

Rupa- kalàpas

Toward the end of the retreat with Ven. Pa Auk Sayadaw, after spending some days on the Four Elements Meditation and progressing to the crystal body, Tina started perceiving a vibrating sensation internally during meditation with eyes closed and externally with eyes open while moving around. This is common once the perception of the crystal body becomes stable, seeing it in block form for at least thirty consecutive minutes of access concentration. At this point, the meditator is instructed to look for the Space Element in the transparent form of the crystal body.

As this practice progresses, the crystal body can suddenly break down into small particles called rupa-kalàpas, which are the smallest subatomic particles of materiality that comprise all matter. Seeing rupa-kalàpas is the final stage of Samatha practice before one begins analyzing the rupa-kalàpas. Analyzing rupa-kalàpas is the first stage of the Vipassana practice, according to the teaching as presented by the Ven. Pa Auk Sayadaw.

In Tina's experience, seeing rupa-kalàpas had a significant and permanent impact on her perception of materiality/physical reality. Having a direct experience of seeing everything one looks at (including one's own body) as moving, sub-atomic particles alters the perception of "me" and of the substantiality of what we take as "normal" reality. Stephen experienced a moment, a very brief flash, of seeing rupa-kalàpas. Due to the limited duration of his experience, it had less of an impact.

It is useful to remember that the traditional description of the Samatha portion of the Buddhist path is described as the "purification of mind," while the Vipassana portion is described as the "purification of view." The internal purification of one's mind stream lays the groundwork for purifying the internal and external "view" of reality as we come to know it as it actually is, rather than as the conditioned mind has taken it to be. Seeing, and later analyzing, rupa-kalàpas is the beginning of seeing materiality as it actually is without the overlay of conceptual thought.

This completes the meditations we have learned under the guidance of Ven. Pa Auk Sayadaw. This book is intended to be used with his book *Knowing and Seeing* to successfully undertake jhâna practice and complete the Samatha portion of the Buddhist path as outlined in the suttas and the *Visuddhimagga*. The experience of the reader may be slightly different than the authors. This is the nature of the solitary journey embarked upon in the purification of mind offered by these ancient practices.

May you experientially know each step
in the footprints of the Buddha
on your path to realizing nibbana.

Tina Rasmussan and Stephen Snyder at the Four Springs Retreat

ABOUT STEPHEN SNYDER

Stephen lived and traveled in Asia as a child and was profoundly affected by the Zen monks he saw as a three-year-old in Tokyo. He began practicing Zen Buddhism in earnest in 1976 at the age of nineteen and has had a daily meditation practice from that time on.

Over the next thirty-plus years, Stephen practiced with several Western Zen masters. He participated in dozens of retreats, receiving several ordinations and the Zen dharma name Hoe' Doetsu ("Peak Wisdom, Mutual Joy"). His primary practices over the years have been the Zen practices of koans and shikantaza, the Tibetan Dzogchen rigpa practice, the Theravada jhânas, and the Diamond Approach. He has also studied with American non-dual teachers.

In 1983, Stephen began law school in order to assist Buddhist Centers as a lawyer in preserving the vessel of the dharma. He went on to work as a practicing lawyer and also served as an advisor to a number of Buddhist and spiritual teachers over the next twenty plus years. During this time he also married and raised two children, who are now thriving adults.

In 1997 he sustained a near-fatal injury. The loss of his career, home, and marriage followed. It was a difficult five-year period of near homelessness, to reclaim his life skill level and rejoin society. His meditation practice and deep intimacy with the dharma was his teacher. In 2004, he met Tina Rasmussen and they were married.

In the meantime, during 2002, Stephen's great friend Robert

Cusick decided to leave his life as a successful sales representative and pursue the life of a Buddhist monk in Burma under the Ven. Pa Auk Sayadaw. Robert's meditative thirst to know the Buddha's jhâna practice struck Stephen deeply. Upon his return to lay life and America, Robert began structuring a Pa Auk jhâna retreat in California during 2005.

Despite having little understanding of jhâna practice, Stephen attended this retreat. His dedication was reflected in his meditating all night one night each week during the retreat. He attained all eight jhânas in the span of the retreat, becoming the first American male to complete this attainment. His life leading up to the retreat had been challenging, yet the purification of mind penetrated thoroughly. He was never the same man. The depth of presence noticed by others since the retreat is contagious. The clearing of deep karma unfolded following this retreat.

Stephen now works as both a lawyer and as a professional and executive coach. He also provides spiritual guidance. For more information, see www.JhânasAdvice.com and www.Enteleky.net.

ABOUT TINA RASMUSSEN

Tina learned to meditate in 1976, at the age of thirteen. Her parents were "spiritually curious" during her teenage years, which opened her to the possibility of mysteries beyond our everyday awareness.

When she was twenty-eight years old, after going through a divorce, Tina started doing silent solo retreats on her own every year. In 1993, she took a vow to meditate for thirty to sixty minutes every single day, which she has done ever since.

In her broader life, her career as an organizational development consultant and coach took off, and she decided to pursue a PhD. At the age of thirty, she was approached by McGraw-Hill and had her first business book published. She moved to the San Francisco Bay Area and started a private consulting practice. Eventually, she became a homeowner, and had a family life with a partner and his son.

At the age of thirty-five, Tina attended her first ten-day Buddhist meditation retreat at Spirit Rock Meditation Center. She sat the one-month retreat at Spirit Rock the following three years, completing numerous ten-day retreats the rest of each year.

At the age of thirty-seven, she realized that worldly accomplishments were becoming less compelling. She became drawn to the idea of having an "urban cave experience" and doing an extended solo retreat at home, rather than traveling to a foreign country to practice at a monastery.

In 2002, she took what seemed like a huge risk given her now single status, self-employment, and mortgage payment, not to mention the sense of identity held in her work. In January of 2003, she began a year-long solo retreat in her condo in Mill Valley, California. During this year, she spent eight to twelve hours a day engaged in spiritual practice. She gave up alcohol, meat, television, entertainment, and (for the most part) talking. She would undertake several weeks or months of silence, seeing or calling friends and family only periodically. The year started with a one-month retreat at Spirit Rock, ended with the three-month retreat at IMS, and was interspersed with the jhânas, Vipassana mindfulness, Tibetan Dzogchen rigpa, the Bramaviharas, yoga and qi gong. In March, she experienced a significant opening, which continued unfolding and deepening for the rest of the year and into the following year.

In 2004, the solo retreat ended and she began the process of integrating the pristine awareness that had developed with the realities of everyday life. Her practice then incorporated aspects of the Diamond Approach, as well as the teachings of American non-dual teachers. In June of 2004, she met Stephen Snyder. They were married in August of 2004.

In March of 2005, Tina and Stephen attended Ven. Pa Auk Sayadaw's jhâna retreat in Middletown, California. Tina ordained as a Theravada Buddhist nun, and Ven. Pa Auk Sayadaw gave her the dharma name of Ayya Pesala ("one whose purity is untarnished by defilements"). During the retreat, Tina became the first American and the first Western woman to complete the eight jhânas (as well as other practices) according to the teachings of Ven. Pa Auk Sayadaw.

Tina now works as a coach and organizational development consultant. She also provides spiritual guidance. For more information, see www.JhânasAdvice.com, www.Enteleky.net, and www.DiversityMosaic.com.